# Jobocalypse

Ben Way

ISBN: 1482701960
ISBN-13: 978-1482701968

# CONTENTS

# ACKNOWLEDGMENTS

Well, I can't believe it. I, a dyslexic*, wrote a book. I am probably as surprised as my elementary school teacher, who once told me that I would never read or write. Before we move onto the topic of robotics, I want to thank a few people who helped me along the way. Without their help, this book would not be possible. Firstly, thank you to my mum and dad. Somehow, a bohemian hippie and a strict accountant lasted long enough together to produce me, and I am forever grateful for that. Thank you to my amazing sister, Hermione Way, for her support and for being with me for part of this journey. I can't wait for her to put her own stories into words one day.

I could not have arrived where I am today without my two amazing adopted families, the Moss and the Williams, who have shown me love and warmth where I expected none.

Thank you to my close friends, Richard Harbutt, Oli Barrett, Chris Saad and Joey Ricard, for putting up with my ramblings over the years.

Thank you to Clara Galán for helping me turn my dyslexic words into something readable, and for working on some of the social media strategy for my book.

*A note to dyslexics: Writing a book is something I never thought I would or could ever do in my life. I have learnt that, with a little help from technology, we can actually be quite good at writing, primarily because we are not constrained by the traditional grammar and spelling perfection that envelopes normal writers. When I first conceived this book, I thought I would need a ghost writer to take my ideas and write them for me. However, I can assure you that not more than around 5% of this book has been rewritten by my editor.

# INTRODUCTION

I can only promise you one thing: robots are going to change your life in ways that you can't even begin to imagine. It is going to happen a great deal sooner than you think. This book provides a front row seat to witness the most exciting, and scariest, ride humanity has ever undertaken: the robotic mechanization of our society. In some sense, it's inevitable. Perhaps it is not something that will come all in one shot, but rather in smaller, bite-sized portions of developments. Once you venture through this book, you will begin to see the groundwork of robotics that has already been and is continually being laid out. Robotic technologies will converge to create more quantum leaps that will ultimately lead to many of the predictions and impending realities of a future; a future of a robotized world. This book will help you to understand the impact that robot mechanization will have not only on your own job, but also on society's workforce as a whole. I will predict how all major industries will be impacted, and provide short and long term predictions for each. However, before we start to explore the future, let me start with the past and my inspiration to write this book.

It was Christmas of 1985. My first experience with a robot was incredible. My robot could walk, talk, tell me bedtime stories and bring me anything I wanted. As his powers were incredible, nothing was too hard for him. We became the best of friends; he would always be there for me, and we lived happily ever after. In reality, I was five years old and had an overactive imagination. Based on the *Tomy Omnibot* television ads I saw, I had imagined my amazing future life with my robot best friend and extremely jealous classmates. For anyone not entirely sure of what an *Tomy Omnibot* is, or rather was, it was a small remote controlled toy robot and the precursor to the i-SOBOT released in 2007 after the merger of the *Tomy* and *Takara* toy companies. Come Christmas day, I looked helplessly for my robotic friend, only to realize that he had been replaced by a book on science. My parents had tried, but never had the money to buy me my robotic friend.

We have been promised robots for generations. When Leonardo da Vinci first imagined his anthrobot over five hundred years ago, he never would have imagined that it would take us so long to master such a simple, yet complicated concept.[1] Now there was an idea, the anthrobot. It only goes to show you the brilliance and genius of da Vinci, who was indeed far ahead of his time. Originally created as a crudely mechanized figure in the form of a human body to prove that human physical actions could be mimicked, the anthrobot was certainly the first of its kind, becoming a proto-invention in a proto-science and technological innovation. It is not as if we have not tried to expand upon da Vinci's initial idea. In fact, NASA is currently researching the anthrobot. The anthrobot is the basis and inspiration for creating a robot that can man the International Space Station and eventually help humanity settle on Mars. It's no coincidence that NASA has termed this new creation in the making as the "anthrobot"; indeed da Vinci's robots were crucial in affecting NASA's own venture into humanistic robotics. After the initial interest in "proto-robotics" in the Renaissance, it was the Industrial Revolution that demonstrated that we could control machines so as long as the task was identical each time. Decades later, the robots we were promised exceeded far beyond the monotonous tasks of the Industrial Revolution. As we watched Star Trek and Star Wars in the latter half of the twentieth century, we learned that robots could actually become our friends, enemies, lovers, and even give humanity freedom from the tyranny of work. We soon began to realize that the invention of robotics was quite possibly either the best or the worst thing that humanity could invent.

The dream of a robotic best friend has never left me since kindergarten. Throughout my childhood, my fascination with robots and mechanics persisted. I was continually armed with a screwdriver and destroyed anything of value in the house, nearly killing myself in the process. My parents often came down in the morning to find me taking apart everything from the main power sockets to the VCR.  I simply liked to refer to the process "repairing" them.

My first real experience with robotics was at school when I was around seven years old. I found out that the big kids had an electronic cupboard in the Science lab. At lunch time I would lock myself in the toilet (that's how popular I was!) with an assortment of electrical components, fetched from the lab, and a vivid imagination. I soon taught myself how the components fit together and began to bring my ideas to life. I built a cardboard floor cleaner with a rudimentary set of commands activated by tinfoil on a cotton spool. This early creation was my first great disappointment in robotics, since my magnificent floor cleaner could not even pick up a paper clip.

My school experience was a recurring theme in my technological education, but not in the traditional sense. Very early on I knew that I was different, not just because I locked myself in toilets with electrical components, but because teachers frequently disciplined me for my rambunctious behavior. My behavior and alternative learning style often caused me to be segregated from the other children. I always knew that I was unlike the other students, but it was not until I was diagnosed with severe dyslexia that I understood the qualities of my learning process and interactions. Dyslexia would become one of the most valuable gifts I had, but it also made my formal educational experience miserable.

When my teachers found out that I was dyslexic, they did not stop exhibiting harsh discipline. However, something else far more important changed. In order to get me out of their hair, my teachers allowed me to sit at the BBC microcomputer system for hours on end by myself without any supervision. Suddenly, I was sitting in front of a piece of technology that did not care whether or not I was dyslexic. The computer would follow and promptly execute my commands without question. My young mind quickly realized that if one could put computers and electronics together, one could build anything.

I thought that robots would give me access to a utopia, but it was not until I was eleven years old that the dark side of robotics entered my consciousness. During my adolescence, I was exposed to the Terminator films, which depicted both the destruction and protection of humanity. These films had a powerful effect on me. They both drove my desire to be in a society full of robots, as well as developed my fear of the potential risks of mechanization. Could robots possibly wipe out humanity?

As I examine this question, I come to the conclusion that nothing is impossible. While I do not think that there is any inherent reason for robots to destroy us, I do think that it is worth analyzing the potential risks and overall impact of robot mechanization. There is a slim chance that robots could destroy humanity, but the impact would be so horrifically devastating that we must attempt to explore the possibility. In reality, one of my projects many years ago was *Weapons Against Robots (or WAR for short),* which was a set of technologies specifically designed for protection against robotic devices. Surprisingly, I was recently contacted about developing the technology for UAVs, Unmanned aerial vehicles, for a defense company. Talk about ahead of the curve! As a species, we are already bracing ourselves for combat with robots.

Over the years, I have kept my dream of developing robots alive. I have taught myself electrical engineering, industrial engineering, kept abreast with the relevant cutting edge technologies, as well as even presented various television programs about them. However, it is only recently that I have recognized that we are about to hit the industry's exponential curve to deliver robots into every part of daily life. While this book primarily explores robotic mechanization's future impact on jobs, the reality is that every aspect of our lives will be changed dramatically in the relatively near future. As we could not have imagined the dramatic impact of the internet over the last decade, it is also difficult for us to anticipate the critical inflection point of robotics in the future. Soon, the world will begin to change in ways that we cannot even begin to imagine.

But, before you think that this book only predicts the future doom and gloom of robotics and the destruction of the workforce as we know it, the true purpose of this book is quite the contrary. Without a doubt, jobs in many industries will fundamentally change in the near future. However, it is the way in which humanity handles these changes that will ultimately determine the outcome of our future. Robots have the capability to create a travesty, or there is the equal possibility that they could usher in an era of human development that frees us to explore our creativity. Personally, I am an optimist. Although I believe that seventy percent of all traditional jobs will disappear within the next thirty years, we can start planning for those changes and challenges now. If we do so, humanity has the opportunity for robots to benefit the many rather than the few.

This is not the first time I have predicted massive changes within industries. During the first wave of the internet, I foresaw the future fundamental changes in the consumer market. Based on my intuition, I developed one of the world's first e-commerce search engines. Unfortunately, my investors felt that I was a disposable asset; however, that is a story for another day. In early 2000, I began to analyze the mobile revolution and saw how it was going to take shape. My predictions brought me to the White House, where I advised the Clinton Administration regarding the transition from analog to digital mobile technology. My experiences at 1600 Pennsylvania Avenue were by far some of the most amazing and proud moments of my life. Hopefully I will have this opportunity again, but on the topic of robotics. However, in other circumstances, some have asked me for advice only to ignore my predictions of disruptive technology. Such included the board of a major music industry label. I warned that their traditional model of physical media distribution would disappear rapidly if they did not prepare for online media sales. Needless to say, they nearly went into bankruptcy forty-eight months later.

So who am I to predict the future? It's not like I have a PhD after my name or any other long string of letters. As a matter of fact, I was written off as a failure by my teachers because of my dyslexia. My backup career was to be a farmer in my small hometown village of Devon, instead of a technologist. I left school at fifteen to start my first business, a computer repair company. It was in business, not school, that I taught myself the fundamentals of technology and its applicability to the consumer market. Over the past two decades, I have immersed myself in business and technology, and have been involved in over one hundred companies spanning across every industry, from solar energy to sex(nothing too naughty I promise), and everything in between. Most of my companies have been technology related using physical technologies. I have built robots as well as artificial intelligence technologies, and I even worked with the UK Ministry of Defense. However, if I disclose too much information about that I would end up in a cell without windows (or OS X!).

Alongside this, I have spent every moment of my life trying to understand the world we live in. This includes not only technology, but also the social, economic and political realities that impact our daily lives. My colleagues describe me as a renaissance man, in that I study the dynamics of our universe in an informal manner driven by interest. At the very least, I am in good company with Einstein, who was both dyslexic and embodied the true nature of a renaissance man.

# CHAPTER 1: THE FUTURE, BACKED UP

Technological revolutions are nothing new, but each revolution comes much more quickly and lasts for a shorter period of time than the previous one. Thus, it always useful to look backwards, in order to understand what lies ahead.

We will never know what initially propelled the first humans to pick up a stone and turn it into a weapon, but it was the miraculous and turbulent beginnings of technology.

The first real revolution began when we learned how to form an agrarian society by implementing resources and working together as a community. We discovered that through farming, we could more efficiently and reliably feed ourselves. This was around 8000BC, but it would be another 9760 years before the next major industrial revolution.[2] Somewhere in our evolution, our brains evolved to the point in which we realized that by taking advantage of natural resources and manipulating them to serve us, it would increase our chances of survival. Ever since then, we have both taken advantage of and abused this evolutionary step. We utilized animals as our engines for hundreds of years and dehumanized our own species to create slavery. However, if you look at the history of robotics, you will also see that the humans started imagining robotics even before we wrote the Bible.

It should come as no surprise that the first conceptual mentions of robotics came from Asia almost two and a half thousand years ago, when a Chinese King wrote about receiving a "mechanical man." Whether or not this encounter actually took place, we will never know. But, given that the mechanical man had all the major organs of a human, the historical account may have been a slight exaggeration. Like ancient China, ancient western history also provides accounts of robotic conceptualization. Aristotle himself once wrote, "There is only one condition in which we can imagine managers not needing subordinates, and masters not needing slaves. This condition would be that each instrument could do its own work, at the word of command or by intelligent anticipation".[3] The Asian trend of robotics continued with the first recorded automated entertainment devices in China and the Middle East around 1000-1200 AD, which included humanoid musicians and chiming clocks. This may have been a far cry from today's idea of a robot, but in the ancient world even a light bulb would have been considered magic.

It was probably Leonardo da Vinci in around 1500 AD that first conceptualized what we would consider a true robot with his *Anthrobot*, a human sized robot knight in shining amour that could sit, stand, move its arm and even open and close its visor. It is not known whether or not Leonardo actually built the *Anthrobot*, but various replicas in the modern world have shown that the basic concepts and ideas were sound.

The Industrial Revolution, like many technological revolutions, was not considered a revolution until it was well under way. From 1830 to 1960, there were a number of simultaneous discoveries and advances in society that led to a critical mass of innovation.[4] Most people of the time period did not realize the Industrial Revolution was occurring until it impacted their lives in unimaginable ways. The same phenomenon will occur during our inevitable robotic revolution.

Massive technological innovations generally bring

unparalleled benefits to humanity. Although the Industrial Revolution forever changed the economic growth and stability for entire populations, there are those who do not view it so. You may have heard of a Luddite, an individual who does not accept new technology and wishes it away. However, the origin of Luddites stems from the Industrial Revolution, during which cotton was spun by hand. It was a manual, strenuous and time consuming process that employed thousands upon thousands of people. One of the first industrial uses of technology was that of the cotton mills, which replaced the thousands of young women working to produce cotton. As they quickly became replaced by technology, those who once held steady jobs found themselves on the street. Without a means to support themselves, most starved and some died. Due to unemployment rates and suffering, the Luddites formed with the primary purpose of destroying technology. The Luddites went to the extremes of destroying cotton mills, which resulted in reinforcements from the British Army in the 1800s.[5]

The Luddites were ultimately misguided. It has been proven again and again that technological revolutions bring about long term economic gains in society. This is due to downwards pressure of replacing low skilled jobs with higher skilled jobs. If technology has been proven to provide economic success over multiple circumstances, you may wonder why we face any risks. You may also question whether or not this book makes the same types of predictions as the Luddites made. However, this book's primary purpose is to explore jobs that are going to be replaced by robots, as opposed to the new jobs that will be created by them.

Despite this, it is important to explore the possibility that these lower skilled jobs will not be replaced. As technology creates new positions in the workforce, lower skilled positions may be eliminated altogether. It is not unreasonable to suggest that there is a requirement for a finite upper number of highly skilled jobs in the future. While the robotic revolution will of course produce new positions of higher expertise, it will be the first time in history in which the technology itself can fulfill some of the new type of jobs that it will create. While I discuss such possibilities, I will also explore some scenarios in the event that these jobs are not replaced.

In order to comprehend the rise of robots, it is important to understand why they are not already a huge part of our lives. Researchers have consistently predicted a robot revolution for the last fifty years, but why has it not yet happened?

To understand this, we need to first look at the brain of a robot, or its processing power. As you will see from the meteoric rise of processing power and the reduction in cost in the graph on the next page, we truly have been following the trajectory set out by Moore in 1965.[6]

We have developed the computing power to control the movement of robots over the last fifty years. Such developments have so far been implemented in large repetitive manufacturing plants that require a robot to perform the same repeated task. This is especially useful in car manufacturing. In reality, the processing power required to make standard repetitive movements is minuscule, as today's digital wrist watches could complete such tasks without a problem.

Thus, if we have the processing power to move a robot in any which way we desire, what holds us back from creating a robot

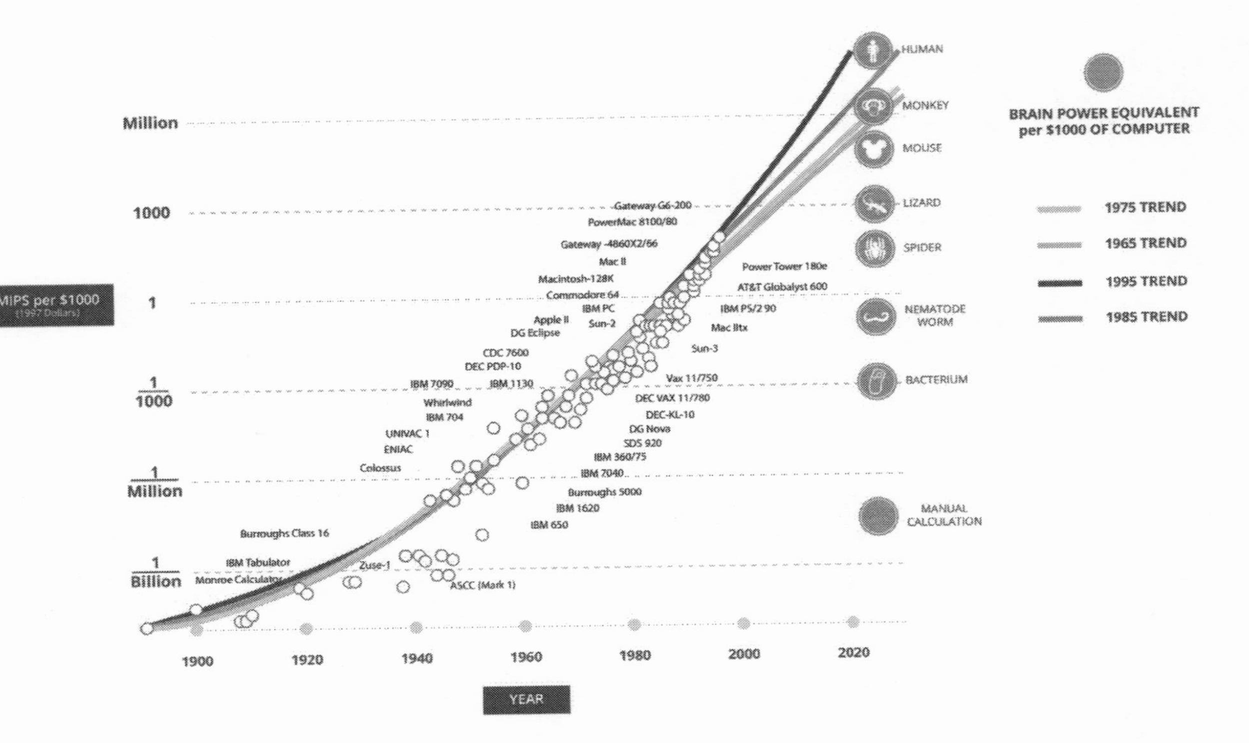
COMPUTING POWER EVOLUTION
MIPS per $1000
(1997 Dollars)
Million
1000
1
1/1000
1/Million
1/Billion
1900
1920
1940
1960
1980
2000
2020
YEAR
HUMAN
MONKEY
MOUSE
LIZARD
SPIDER
NEMATODE WORM
BACTERIUM
MANUAL CALCULATION
BRAIN POWER EQUIVALENT per $1000 OF COMPUTER
1975 TREND
1965 TREND
1995 TREND
1985 TREND
Gateway G6-200
PowerMac 8100/80
Gateway -4860X2/66
Mac II
Macintosh-128K
Commodore 64
IBM PC
Sun-2
Apple II
DG Eclipse
CDC 7600
DEC PDP-10
IBM 7090
IBM 1130
Whirlwind
IBM 704
UNIVAC 1
ENIAC
Colossus
Burroughs Class 16
IBM Tabulator
Monroe Calculator
Zuse-1
ASCC (Mark 1)
Power Tower 180e
AT&T Globalyst 600
IBM PS/2 90
Mac IItx
Sun-3
Vax 11/750
DEC VAX 11/780
DEC-KL-10
DG Nova
SDS 920
IBM 360/75
IBM 7040
Burroughs 5000
IBM 1620
IBM 650

that completes every task we want it to? One issue is mobility, which will later be discussed, but the most important issue is the authentic dynamic environment to which robots still find it very difficult to adapt and interact with. While a robot can perform repetitive tasks, or NASA likes to put it, “Robots tend to perform as well or better than humans when the tasks and conditions can be reliably predicted”, it is woefully underpowered when it encounters authentic changing environments and tasks.[7] It is only recently that processing power has been available for us to effectively replicate our basic senses. In order for robots to make a profound impact in our world, they must be able to understand, process, and react to the variations of the surrounding environment.

Although robots face this difficulty, there are an emerging number of technologies that that are turning robotic environment processing into a reality. Many of these technologies have grown out of the mobile phone revolution, which has pushed a substantial increase in high quality, low cost microelectronics over the last ten years. The first of such microelectronics was that of low cost, high-resolution cameras that allowed low cost three-dimensional stereo vision. The first robots with three-dimensional stereo vision began to perceive depth, an extremely important ability for performing complex tasks in a dynamic environment. Imagine trying to navigate through a crowded space using only a two dimensional view and the challenges that the camera’s limited vision provides.

When *Google* began to develop the self-driving car, the company needed a technology with more accurate vision to gather precise images. *Google* opted to use LIDAR, a fancy acronym representing a laser that finds objects in the range of a

360 degree arc. The full form of it is "Light Detection and Ranging" or "Laser Imaging Detection and Ranging". Think about LIDAR as an extremely fast spinning lighthouse that illuminates everything in its path, and carries the cost of several thousand digital cameras.

Needless to say, a good deal of these technologies, as well as the technologies to intelligently interpret them, will combine with the currently available processing power to make the "thinking and sensing" side of robotics relatively simple. This leads us onto the two real problems with current robotics technology, power and movement. The power problem is exactly the same as that of a mobile phone. As processing power of a mobile phone over time has increased, battery technology has unsuccessfully tried to keep up. Presently, in order to power a decently large robot for consistent useful work, it must be either tethered to the mains power or powered by a mechanical engine that generates power. There are huge advances in technology in this area, the first being improved battery technology. Even though batteries unfortunately do not follow Moore's law, they do increase their performance by around 5% a year. Secondly, we are making computers more efficient with the available energy.[8] The other developing area is that of fuel cells that are just beginning to make their way into consumer products. Fuel cells will transform natural gas into water in one compact unit with the benefit of generating significant electrical energy from an energy dense fuel.

Evidently, a large number of the technologies that will be required for the robotic revolution are already nearly in place. So, what is missing? Well, it is really quite simple. We have yet to invent a better, more efficient, more compact, cheaper means of generating movement than the humble electric motor invented in 1821.[9] This simple device is responsible for *servo*, a device that can accurately move in a circular 360 degree arc for driving gears or wheels. Motors are relatively heavy, large and inaccurate for the fine movements that robotics require.

It is not as if we have not tried to come up with a better solution for generating robotic movement. All sorts of actuators, motors that turn energy into motion, have been tested. Some have been quite successful in their narrow field of use. Hydraulic actuators have been used in industrial robots that require great strength, while air actuators have been implemented in more delicate settings. However, one will encounter each actuator's strengths and significant weaknesses when trying to build ubiquitous robots.

Thus, in order to try and solve the limitations of actuators, some very clever scientists are working with advanced materials. We now have artificial muscles that can contract in the presence of electro-active polymers, basically electricity, or heat. Even though some of these new technologies can deliver relatively strong responses at low energy levels, the amount they actually contract is not enough to perform useful work. I suspect that once these new materials mature, they will indubitably drive the robotic revolution forward. Humanity is a good ten years away from this new technology's incorporation into products, but when it is entirely incorporated by then, the face of robotics will be forever changed. It is fascinating that a number of these technologies have been inspired by biology. We must not forget that the human body is an incredible device. While we may lament that we do not have the robots that we were promised for hundreds of years, we are well on our way to replicating that which biology has been perfecting for millions of years.

However, even without these technologies, the robotic revolution is slowly but surely creeping up on us. In the USA alone, the robotics company *iRobot* has sold over 7.5 million robots to consumers and Japan Robot Association predicts that in ten years home robot sales will increase by over 250%.[10] But, those numbers really don't do the industry justice. The reality is that the robotics industry will follow the accelerated growth curves that the internet and the mobile industry enjoyed. As you can see on the next page, exponential growth is already occurring.

After all, although wireless communication has been around for decades, it was only when it hit the tipping point that explosive growth truly and naturally occurred. Also, I believe that each time a technological revolution commences, it advances at a quicker pace than the previous one. As soon as techies, industry and recreational users realize the true potential of the robotic revolution, investment in and development of the technology will eclipse anything we have ever seen before.

"Okay, great. So we may be creating more robots and they're going to revolutionize our lives and the world at large. But why and how will this affect jobs?" you may ask. Surely I am just making the same mistakes as the Luddites and others who predicted that computers and the internet would destroy the jobs we have now. Well, firstly, technology has a measurable effect on the employment situation, which I call "unemployment slack."

"Unemployment slack" refers to the extended period of time it takes for employment rates to recover from an economic recession.

Obviously, each recession and moment in history has its

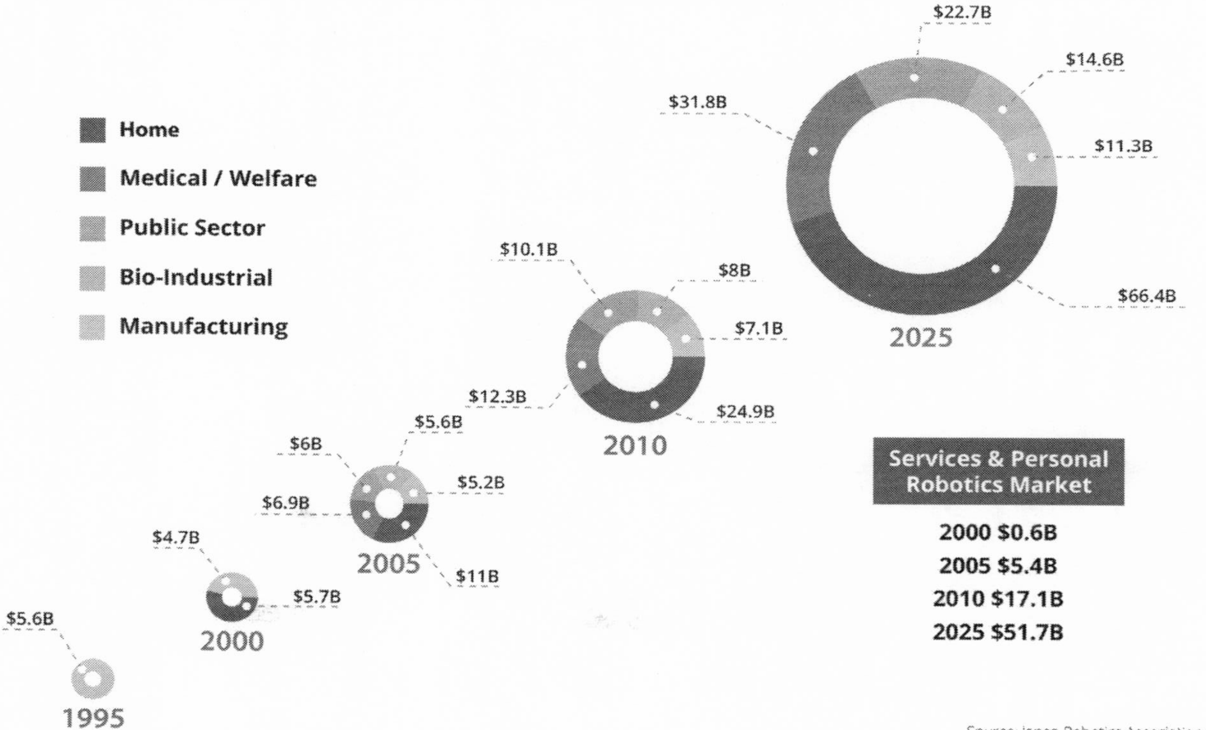
ROBOT INDUSTRY PREDICTED GROWTH
Home
Medical / Welfare
Public Sector
Bio-Industrial
Manufacturing
$5.6B
1995
$4.7B
$5.7B
2000
$6B
$5.6B
$6.9B
$5.2B
$11B
2005
$10.1B
$8B
$7.1B
$12.3B
$24.9B
2010
$22.7B
$14.6B
$31.8B
$11.3B
$66.4B
2025
Services & Personal Robotics Market
2000 $0.6B
2005 $5.4B
2010 $17.1B
2025 $51.7B
Source: Japan Robotics Association

own unique set of circumstances. There are a number of different theories that address why technology has not affected employment as much as many would theorize it should. Erik Brynjolfsson and Andrew McAfee from MIT conjecture that technology has already had a massive impact on jobs by creating stagnation of median income. Their theory states that while technology has allowed for productivity gains, it has not increased in line with the jobs that should have been generated by those gains.

However, like most things in life, the answer is not black and white. The reason why we have not seen the massive effects on employment is probably due to a number of factors. I am a great believer in *Occam's Razor,* which states that all things being equal, the simplest explanation is normally the right one. Based on my experiences in numerous businesses, the statistics on employment slack graph on the next page parallel the simple reality of commercial employment.

During an economic boom, employers hire candidates slightly before they need to so that the company stays ahead of growth. Even an inefficient staff becomes valuable due to the tacit knowledge of an organization's behavior. So, why spend the management time trying to weed out the inefficiencies when an employer could be using the same time to grow the company? More often than not, the organization becomes lazy and finds it easier to stay with the status quo than to constantly achieve optimum efficiency. The old adage, "if it ain't broke, don't fix it," becomes a mantra for all issues from the technology department to human resources. In fact, I have seen so many conversations between the CEO and the CTO of a company go something like this during good economic times:

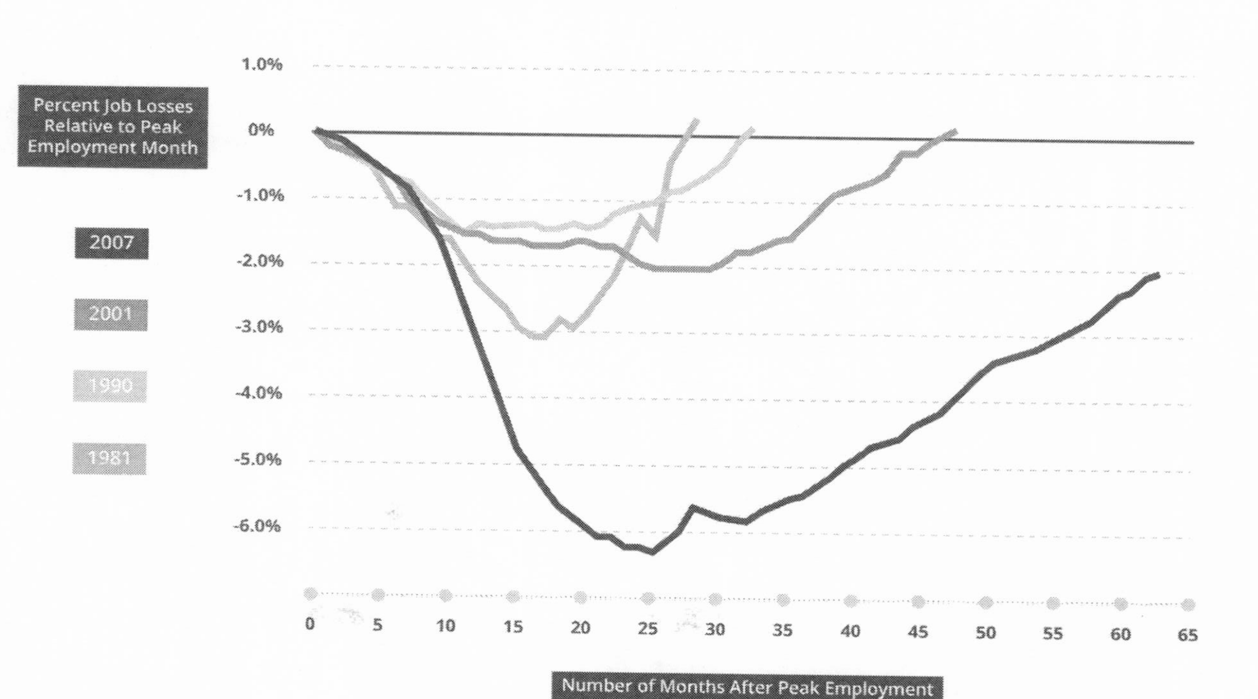
EMPLOYMENT SLACK
Percent Job Losses Relative to Peak Employment Month
2007
2001
1990
1981
1.0%
0%
-1.0%
-2.0%
-3.0%
-4.0%
-5.0%
-6.0%
0
5
10
15
20
25
30
35
40
45
50
55
60
65
Number of Months After Peak Employment
http://www.calculatedriskblog.com/

CEO: "I have seen this new amazing technology. If we implemented it, it could save us millions."

CTO (*Deep intake of breath*): "We could implement it, and it could save us the money, but the system integration could take years. Then, this new technology could have problems integrating into our older systems. I'd be happy to do it, but I can't give you an accurate cost or timeline. How would you like me to proceed?"

CEO: "Okay, well why don't we review it in six months?"

The reality is that most new technologies usually can be implemented relatively easily within a decent timeframe and cost. In a recession, on the other hand, the conversation between CEO and CTO goes much more like this:

CEO: "I have seen this amazing new technology. If we implemented it, it could save us millions."

CTO (*Deep intake of breath*): "We could implement it, and it could save us the money, but the system integration could take years. Then, this new technology could have problems integrating into our older systems. I'd be happy to do it, but I can't give you an accurate cost or timeline. How would you like me to proceed?"

CEO: "Okay, but I need you to know that we are cutting our operating budget significantly and your department will have to be downsized. We need to find a way to cut costs."

CTO: "Well, it is going to be tough, but I think I can implement it. I will put together a budget and timeline for our next board meeting."

The above dialogues are an example of the *Nash Equilibrium*, in which most people will work for their own interests, as well as the interests of the group as a whole. During an economic boom, the CTO wants to exert the least amount of effort for the maximum reward without harming the rest of the organization. The easiest way for a CTO to do this is to avoid introducing new technology that will require extra work. Not taking action makes the CTO's job easier, and he or she can justify the decision by claiming that it is in the best interest of the company. Lack of action and new technologies eliminates the risk of failure and the cost of introduction.

However, during an economic depression, the balance shifts and it is in the CTO's interests (i.e. status, salary bonus, maintaining position in the company) to implement new cost-effective technologies. The introduction of new technology is also in the interest of the whole company through reduction of layoffs and increased revenue. Due to these factors, the CTO finds a way to implement new cost-effective technologies.

The above scenario is repeated in thousands of organizations, and it is that cost saving momentum which drives new technology adoption in large slowly moving organizations. Each time industry goes through this cycle, it takes a longer period of time for unemployment rates to lower because technology has replaced many positions. At some point, as some economists believe, it will be impossible to return to the same low level of unemployment.[11] Some argue that we have already reached that point.[12]

Another trend that exhibits the impact of technology on our efficiency is the average hours a week that the average employee works. Work hours have been declining steadily and have been reduced by 7% since the massive growth of the personal computer in 1980s.[13]

It is important to note that these numbers do not take into account the shadow labor market of illegal immigrants. One only has to analyze the near zero net immigration from Mexico in the last few years to realize that it has had a much bigger impact on the US labor market than any other source.[14] Taking illegal immigration into consideration, the reduction of jobs is most likely much worse than officials would lead us to believe.

Thus, during each recession, the "unemployment slack" takes over a longer period of time and our working week slowly reduces. Low-level positions are always replaced with that of higher skills, as we have seen in every other technological revolution. So, why is the robotic revolution different? Well, in every other technological revolution, a low-level job has generally been replaced with a position that requires higher skills. For example, cotton workers gave way to mechanics, while secretarial work was eventually taken over by programmers. In general, this has contributed to higher wages, which in turn has driven consumption. Such circumstances lift the quality of life and economic success of almost all people.

However, robots are different in a number of ways. Firstly, robots will be the first technology in history that will be able to build themselves. Robots that can build other robots may sound scary, but this certainty will be the reality of the robotic industry. However, to dispel any fears at this point, it would be safe to say that although these robots would be able to build other robots and implement a more advanced "learning mode of thinking", their ability to "evolve" into terminator type entities would always be limited by the processing power of their processors. In other words, it will be more than likely that these robots may have "evolutionary" chips that will help them to learn new skills, just as the brain creates neural pathways when learning new concepts. However, the power of these chips will be limited in comparison to human minds. Then again, you never know, technology moves very fast! If robots can acquire new skills through "evolutionary" chips, then who's to say that they wouldn't be able to just build themselves more powerful processing chips with increased memory and the ability to gain enhanced skills and knowledge? Secondly, robots can repair themselves without human interaction. In the most extreme cases, a robot will be able to diagnose itself, and only a select number of human operators will repair or replace the robot's parts. Of course, if we were to take into account the possibility of the malleable and extendable "evolutionary" chips, the need for human implementation in fixing the robot would be virtually non-existent. Thirdly, while most technological revolutions provided expand knowledge and improve skill for the industry they revolutionize, robotics within itself will not require much more additional engineering knowledge than a programmer or an electrical engineer already possesses. In other words, our brains have limitations in knowledge and understanding, and I believe we are nearing that limit. Robotics and technology is the only means of surpassing the limitations of human mind power. Indeed, the means of surpassing this limit is only limited by the extent of resources available for furthering a robot's knowledge, be they human limitations of programming that robot or scarcity or rarity of materials. Fourthly, we live in a disposable society and robots are increasingly disposable and easily replaceable as costs decrease. This trend will continue in the future as the cost of replacing robots and repairing them becomes virtually the same. We tend not to repair mechanical or hardware technology, and instead prefer to replace it instantly with a new version.

Thus far, most technology simply has changed the way we work through higher efficiency, but it has not replaced us completely. For example, accountants were not completely replaced by calculators, but rather the calculators made the accountants more efficient. The most challenging aspect of robots is that they will work from the bottom of the low skill level jobs upwards in a very short period of time. This is the most troubling aspect of technology because robots can immediately replace low-level employees with the least economic stability. This, in turn, places a huge burden on the welfare state. However, as I will allude to in the later chapter on health, this burden may well be offset by the massive advantages of cost reductions in care for the aging population.

So, what will be the effects on our society? Well, that is yet to be determined by human reactions and the rate in which the robotic revolution comes to pass. I suspect that we will see the first direct effects of the revolution on the lowest skilled jobs and illegal immigrants. Next, the impact will start moving up the chain. Job sector after job sector will soon be replaced, until only the most creative and taxing jobs remaining will be completed by humans. However, the robotic revolution does not need to be the future doom and gloom for our society. Even though I suspect that there will be an extended time of turbulence in society, as society adjusts to these changes, it could eventually allow us to reach our ultimate creative potential as a species and drive a new renaissance period.

What could the future look like? There are two likely scenarios depending on how we approach the change politically, economically and socially. The worst-case scenario is a precarious drop in employment to the point where the majority of the population becomes unemployed. This, in turn, will create a two class system that could potentially eliminate the middle class as we know it. Those who obtain the economic means or skills set that a robot cannot replicate will find their standard of living ever increasing as robots provide a level of luxury and service that will only be available to the wealthiest of individuals in today's world.

Individuals who cannot afford the luxuries of robots will live in abject poverty. This poverty will consist of micro living spaces combined with advances in immersive virtual worlds. Such virtual reality will provide the lower class of society a life with limited external social interaction or experiences. This may sound farfetched, but if you already look at the trends in certain demographics, it is already occurring. Every year, a more significant number of people spend the majority of their time in a virtual world as opposed to reality. With the onset of massive multiplayer online role-playing games, social networks like *Facebook* and *Twitter*, and the increased availability of TV shows and movies over the Internet, the trend of people spending more time in front of a screen as opposed to other recreational activities is the future reality. I daresay it is already a fixed reality that will be further coalesced by declining employment rates and a larger gap between the "haves" and "have-nots". Ironically, even the have-nots would have access to the virtual worlds and advanced technology, a reality once considered science fiction, and even luxurious, only twenty to thirty years ago. Eventually these real worlds will become so close to reality that the quality of life within these virtual worlds will exceed much of the true life quality of the lower socioeconomic class.

The other and best case scenario is that governments adapt quickly to these changes and provide the education and support that the unemployed will need to move up the skills ladder. The challenge is that it will cause a significant amount of employment excess, and it is unlikely that the employment sponge, i.e. the economy, will be able to react quickly enough to provide the level of employment required. In this case, I foresee that, due to political or general changes in society, there will be a downward pressure to decrease the hours of the work week. Flexible hours, or a two to three day work week, would absorb some of the excess labor and create the social benefit of freeing people to explore their creative sides. This could in turn open up a new Renaissance Period, where people will focus less on money and more on the human journey of life. Humanity also may live a much better quality of life and engage in philanthropy. One only has to look to the Mediterranean cultures of "siestas" and family gatherings to know that life should not be all about work.

In either scenario there is one big problem. We are a society of consumption, a self-feeding beast that drives the economy forward. Based on the history of recessions, the significant rise of unemployment levels has a massive detrimental effect on an economy and the tax revenues that sustain that economy. As the unemployed population grows, the greater the burden becomes on the social welfare system and taxpayers.

However, there could be one saving grace for a robotically-driven economy. If an economy is driven by free energy (renewable resources) and a vast section of inefficiency in government is replaced by robotics (military, health care, education), as well as much cheaper goods driven by factories (or 3D printers), the only cost would be that of raw materials and energy. When the robotic workforce is effectively free, we may find ourselves in a situation in which material goods and the cost of running our economy rapidly decreases in line with the decline in the workforce.

Ultimately, I am an optimist. While I do expect there to be some pain through this process, the end result could be a civilization that is unburdened by material goods and that allows every single citizen to live a fantastic quality of life.

There will be those who look at the evidence and draw different conclusions, but inherently, most people know that robotic technology will eventually have a fundamental impact on jobs. It's like global warming. It has been predicted for over a hundred years that we are making a fundamental impact on the environment around us. The predicted tipping point of catastrophe from global warming has come and gone several times over the past one hundred years. Each time humanity has passed that predicted tipping point, the data has been used to discredit the theory of global warming. Now, as we are starting to live with the consequences of global warming, it is obvious that we are within the tipping point.[15] The same is true for robotics. Over the past century, we have predicted that this technology will change our lives, but robotics has yet to make the profound impact that many have predicted. However, this does not mean that this impact will not occur in the imminent future. What I see now is a combination of varying and virtually infinite trends that show me we are truly at the tipping point of our robotic future, and I do not hesitate to predict its coming.

# CHAPTER 2: ODD JOBS

Illegal immigrants are amazing. We fail to appreciate them, but they are responsible for many of the services we take for granted. They operate at such a low cost that to remove them from the economy would drive up prices for almost everything. It would also lower our comfortable standard of living and attack our quality of life.

However, illegal immigrants' greatest benefit to the economy is that of providing low-cost labor for low skilled jobs. Of course, I'm generalizing here; there are both very skilled legal and illegal immigrants. Such low-cost labor is also the Achilles' heel of illegal immigration. Low-cost/low skilled labor will be the first to be replaced by robots, thus eliminating many jobs for illegal immigrants. The first wave of consumer robots will be crude and functional at best, as they will only be able to perform repetitive tasks in relatively stable surroundings. Anyone who has played with an *iRobot* vacuum cleaner or a robotic lawnmower can attest that it will become stuck with the simplest objects in its way. Unless the obstacle is removed, the robot is useless. Don't even fantasize about the robotic vacuum cleaner being able to clean up the stairs. Robots that can perform monotonous tasks are the reason that illegal immigrants and very low-skill level workers will be the first to suffer at the hands of a robotic revolution. It is already occurring now. How many people have replaced a maid with a robotic *Hoover*, a gardener with a robotic lawnmower or the pool cleaner with a robotic pool cleaner? Given the nature of this segment of the population, it is very hard to know the statistics as the low skilled labor records become harder to find due to under-the-table dealings with such labor. There is no doubt that illegal immigrants will be the first to feel the coming of the robotic revolution. For the first time in recent history, Mexican immigration has been at a standstill with over 1.3m Mexicans leaving the USA between 2005-2010 mostly due to the economic recession[14]. This is a sign of the times to come. I'm not saying that robotic replacements are the sole reason for their departure, but it is indeed an influential factor in a myriad of other factors, which include not only a decline in standard of living for illegal immigrants in the economic recession, but also an increase in the prospects of work and standard of living in these immigrants" native countries.

Initially, robots will be introduced alongside their human counterparts. For example, an industrial robotic floor cleaner will be wiping the floor at *McDonald's,* as the janitor executes more complicated tasks such as wiping down tables or cleaning the cooking machinery. However, as robots can attack more and more complicated simultaneous tasks over time, there will come a point in which janitors will not be able to make themselves look busy for the entire day. Full-time work will transition into part-time work.

One of the misconceptions that occurs when people think about robots taking over their jobs is that they almost always imagine a humanoid robot. Humanoid robots will emerge in the distant future, but the robots that will replace most jobs will be specialist machines for specific odd jobs. For example, if you have a blocked toilet, you can down a snake-like robot to explore the drains and remove the blockage (I certainly hope this comes with a self-cleaning function). If you want your windows washed, a small portable flying robot will do the job. These robots will not necessarily be as fast as humans, but they will be reliable. Once the initial cost of these robots has been paid, they will work for free without maintenance for a very long period of time. The speed of robots also does not matter as much as one may believe. A flying window cleaning robot, for example, may only clean one pane at a time before going to back to recharge and add extra fluid. But, it can work 24 hours a day, 365 days a year if you want it to. It is completely automated. Imagine a few flying window cleaning bots on every skyscraper in the world. The impact this would have on window cleaners would wipe out their work opportunities entirely. In reality, this technology is not that far away, as it is one of the technologies that my solar company is developing.

There are some low skill tasks, however, that even advanced robots will find difficult. Most of these tasks include an exponential number of variables, as well as a good measure of unpredictability. It may very well take a human only a short amount of time to master the skill of ironing and folding, but the task is a robot's worst nightmare. It is extremely challenging for a robot to understand what the clothing is, the clothing's material and the variance of the way the material falls. Approaching the task of ironing and folding would make the most advanced robot known to man look as useful as the offspring of a BBC micro and a washing machine. Although, both an ironing robot and a folding robot are actually in the process of being developed. I have seen a robot fold a shirt in front of me at the *FoldiMate* headquarters, and I can assure you that even the prototype does it better than a human can. When products like the folding and ironing robots are launched, the companies clearly feel that there is a demand in the market, even with the limitations of the current technology. Perhaps, that's rightly so; I mean who likes to fold and iron clothes anyway?

However, it is unlikely that consumers will be the first to adopt robots. Apart from consumers being much fussier and demanding, they would also probably wait until to purchase a robotic product until it is both popular and cost-effective. Commercial applications can be easily and economically justified, even if there is a high cost upfront. The auto industry is a good example of this, as they already rely heavily on robotic installations to replace low-skilled labor. Individuals in the auto industry can easily bear the millions of dollars of investment required to try a new robot, because they know that over the long term, these robots will pay for themselves a hundred times over. Advanced consumer robots, on the other hand, are likely to be initially expensive, unreliable and have bugs. I expect them to become a status symbol for the very rich, and until they mature and develop, they will likely be placed into a niche market for some time. They will also require similar leasing options as cars have today to obtain real traction in the market.

Within the next generation, the humanoid robots that we see in films such as *I, Robot* will find their way into our homes and will be able to perform almost any task more efficiently and better than any human ever could. At this point, there is very little hope for casual labor to exist.

But one of the questions that will determine if these robotic helpers will replace their human counterparts is whether or not society accepts these faceless drones occupying their homes. Won't it be strange to come home to a robot that occupies your personal space and responds to your every request, but lacks a personality? However, these robots will have personalities.

Robotic companies will not build their technologies in isolation and the best robot manufacturers will need to understand the psychology behind robot and human interactions. This is already evident with Apple's *Siri.* Apple did not choose a sexless drone-like voice to meet the demands of iPhone users. Instead, Apple tried to give *Siri* a personality so that consumers could connect with her on an emotional level. If we can connect with technology emotionally, we are more likely to forgive it when it makes mistakes or goes wrong. Apple has actually employed special writers to give *Siri* this special emotional edge. While I am not in love with *Siri,* and in most cases find her completely useless, her witty retorts do ease my frustrations. While the face of this home-helper robotics will not be human-like for a long period of time, they will employ facial expressions to engage and drive emotional responses. We should expect exaggerated responses from the first human android home robots, much like is present in the film *Short Circuit,* which creates the main character's personality in a cold steel body. We won't see robots that are trying to mimic human facial appearance exactly for quite some time. Karl F. MacDorman coined the term "uncanny valley" to describe the way in which humans feel deeply uneasy when presented with a robot that does not respond in the expected way a human would. The reason behind this is that robots are sometimes slightly off when trying to replicate human behavior, like micro expressions. Unlike robots, human beings have a specific set of neurons that help us to predict other human behavior during interactions. When robots fail to recognize and match our unconscious expectations, we feel uncomfortable. However, this technology will rapidly develop and the most number of advancements, unsurprisingly, will most likely come from the sexbots industry, which I will cover in a later chapter.

It is important not just to think about the changes robots will bring about in isolation, but also the emerging robotic technology combined with advanced materials and 3D printing. Such emerging technology will have the biggest impact on our society. Rather than simply replacing a part of a process, this new technology can revolutionize it. Although there is the possibility of a brick-laying robot in the future of construction, chances are that with 3D printing on a grand scale, buildings will rise out of the ground automatically with robotic technologies putting in the finishing touches. This is not as farfetched as it might sound, as the first 3D printed buildings are already under construction.[16]

When those buildings become big enough, they will be manned by a robotic staff. This scenario has already occurred, and a good friend of mine and fellow entrepreneur, Simon Woodroffe, is the first person to implement robotic bag handlers in his flagship hotel, *yotel,* in Times Square.[17] While some may find robotic bag handlers gimmicky, it is just a start of the transition to an all robotic staff. Remember when hotels had elevator operators? Me neither.

Another segment of the odd job category would be that of the municipal job segment. You only have to stand in line at the DMV to understand that robots could easily replace humans in a great deal of government organizations. However, it will most likely be the municipal and government institutions that take the longest to adopt the technology, partly because they are generally slow at adopting new technology and partly because there will be a great deal of pressure from unions. Municipal jobs that are outsourced to private contractors, on the other hand, will most likely be the first to go.

It does not take a lot of effort to apply some of the technologies we have already talked about to municipal tasks. Garbage trucks already use robotic tongs to grab garbage cans, and by applying self-driving technology, we can create the wonderful driverless garbage truck.[18] It also won't take long before small UAVs can trim trees, water plants and even paint over graffiti (which the rouge graffiti bots will probably have painted in the first place). [19]

However, everything won't be perfect for citizens. Just like automated speed cameras have been abused to generate revenue, the all-seeing eyes of the municipal bots will most likely prove to be too invasive. The only redeeming quality that will make parking bots bearable is the fact that all the parking inspectors will lose their jobs because of them!

Overall though, the robotic revolution in municipals should bring major cost reductions and better, cleaner streets and parks, while tasks like street cleaning, pavement repair and park maintenance all become automated. This is the just beginning of the possibilities of the robot revolution. The revolution will change the face of our society, economy, and possibly even our mental and emotional framework. Humanity will become more and more used to such changes, which in turn will free up our time to pursue more humanistic and creative activities.

# CHAPTER 3: ADULT INDUSTRY AND HOW TO EJECT SAFELY

Sex. If there is anything that makes us human, it is our burning evolutionary desire to mate. It has been suggested that the whole of humanity's achievements have developed so that we could impress the opposite sex and mate with the best possible genetics. I wouldn't go quite that far, but there is no doubt that sex drives a huge amount of human activity.

Technology has partly been driven by sex. From the earliest days technology has been used to fulfill our desires and drive our imaginations. It is said that a lot of the internet technologies we take for granted these days were driven by the consumer demand for naked pictures and now video down the proverbial pipe. But sex and robots? Do they really mix?

Not only do they mix, they were meant to be together. Sex is such a messy, dangerous, complicated and amazing activity that we spend huge amounts of resources and energy to engage in. Rarely are we satisfied in terms of quality or quantity, and the way in which the two sexes like to engage in sexual behavior is almost at the opposite end of spectrum--most males opt to spread their seeds far and wide, while women trying to encourage men to engage in a long-term monogamous relationship.

Technology has already changed the face of relationships beyond recognition. Just a few generations ago we were expected at a young age to find one partner and settle down for the rest of our lives. This resulted in a predictable result of a divorce rate that has been steadily rising for decades.

It's not that we did not try hard. It's just that the construct of marriage was primarily driven by society, not our biology, and thus at some point was destined to be doomed. In fact, for most, the history of marriage was a control mechanism for men to "own" a woman, and until the 20th century, having mistresses and lovers or visiting prostitutes was a common activity for a married man, even if it was never talked about.[20]

Don't get me wrong. I want to experience the sanctity of marriage, but I also know that unless something changes or I am extremely lucky in being in the 50% of marriages that do not end in divorce, my biological desire to mate with everything in a skirt does not match my mental desires of wanting a family and a wife.[21, 22]

Robots could be the answer to a lot of the challenges we face, but the true questions would revolve around how long it would take for society to change its entrenched views on its perceived morality.

Pornography is evil; well that's what we have been told for the last century since it's been around in its accessible form. It has only been over the last thirty years that society has become more liberal, and we now accept that porn can be part of a healthy relationship. In fact, in today's generation you would almost be weird if you did not experience pornography, so it has become accepted as a healthy normal part of relationships.[23]

Vibrators are also evil; or that's how they were perceived when they started appearing thirty years ago. In fact, they were so "wrong" that they had to be marketed as massage devices for decades. But again, attitudes have changed these mechanical devices, which now come in a dizzying array of forms and are probably in most western homes, not as devices of shame but as devices of pleasure.

So, if pornography and vibrators were evil and now are a common part of a healthy relationship, could sex bots do the same? The big challenge to sex bots becoming part of a healthy relationship is actually one that you might not imagine; it is likely we will be able to fall in love with our bots. Yes, that's right. Humans have been designed to build emotions and connections with objects we covet since primate evolution began.

We are ridiculous in this regard, but it serves multiple biological and evolutionary benefits starting with the bond to one's mother; but we build these bonds regardless of whether or not the object of our appreciation is human, animal or inanimate, and now possibly robotic or artificial intelligence. Just think of the number of people who name their car, covet their mobile device or would be devastated if their pet died.

So, if we have the ability to love things, why not a robot? Well, in fact, we are more likely to fall in love with robots because they will be designed to have personalities that reflect our own. Studies have already shown these connections and there is already a name for it *Lovotics.*[24] As robots become more like humans in appearance and behavior, we will feel more and more connected to them.

These changes are already happening in society. You only have to look at the success of *Real Doll* which has developed almost indistinguishable human sex dolls with every possible characteristic you can imagine.[25] Also technologies to bring couples and strangers together through technology are becoming available, such as the *Mojowijo* that allows you to transmit the feelings of one vibrator into another across any distance using the internet.[26]

But this is just the beginning. Sex bots are coming. What does that mean for the adult industry?

Well, let's start with the good stuff. Once sexbots really can replicate the real act of sex, it won't take long for the illegal sex trafficking trade to take a big hit. These forced jobs will not make economic sense when sexbot brothels or sexbot renting start appearing. This appalling underbelly of human exploitation will take a significant hit, maybe to the point where authorities can actually start to crack down and make a difference in dismantling it.

It will also start to erode the business models of pornography. There are not many people who would choose porn over the real thing, so if sexbots do become an acceptable part of society, it is likely that a great deal of the content created will become a niche. Additionally, with the type of restrictions that California is already imposing on the porn industry, in the near future there is the possibility that robot sex porn will be the only acceptable form of pornography for health and safety reasons.

Prostitutes will also find the robotic revolution a challenging environment to ply their trade. With bot sex freely available and cheap, the incentives of sleeping with a human will become significantly diminished. The world's oldest, and arguably the most stable, industry could get wiped out in terms of its labor force by being replaced by robots.

So, how far away are we from sexbots? Well, basic mechanical sex machines exist today but you could hardly call them robots[26]. Personally, I wouldn't be surprised if within the next ten years we start seeing more sophisticated sexbots that can respond and move in basic ways. In another twenty years, I suspect that for sex purposes you will not know the difference between a sexbot and human, and you will be able to have sexbots in every shape, size, sex or even any fantasy you can imagine.

This also brings up the moral questions that governments should start thinking about now. As awful as it is to think about, there will be a demand for child or animal sexbots. Do we allow these on the basis that it could stop the abuse of real living humans? Or, is it more likely to drive dangerous and perverted behavior? It's a question I can't even begin to answer, and it is probably best left to psychologists to determine and governments to decide how to approach this. I just hope they start thinking about the issue now before technology overtakes them.

# CHAPTER 4: LOGISTICS WITH HARD DRIVES

The driverless car is upon us. You may not be able to buy one quite yet, but *Google*'s self-driving cars have been whizzing around California for the past few years and have clocked up 300,000 miles without any crashes.[27] Actually, one of the *Google* cars did receive a fender bender, but it was only due to a human who was in control of the car. It's one point for the robots and zero for humanity.

We are already used to driverless vehicles, so the transition to driverless cars should not be challenging for the average human. Do you worry when you go on one of the mass transport driverless systems in airports? Even the L New York Subway line is now driverless.[28] You probably don't even give mass transport a second thought because it's normal and everyone else uses it. It's the future; sit back and enjoy the ride.

Initially, the driverless automated technology will be only in luxury cars, and will require a "backup" driver at all times. You know, just in case the robotic technology fails. However, as soon as people are comfortable with a hands-off approach to driving and the fact that it is likely to be significantly safer than the human equivalent, the pressure will mount to remove humans from the equation. The first arguments will be around drunk driving. As people feel more confident in their car's ability to drive itself, they are likely to take bigger and bigger risks. The self justification will be easy after a few drinks. I mean how easy is it to say to yourself, "it's a better driver than me when I am sober, so imagine how much better it is when I am drunk!" As this pressure grows, there will be the realization that tens of thousands of lives could be saved just by allowing the self-driving cars to do what they do best: drive themselves.

With this technology available to the consumer in less than five years, it won't take long before automobile industry wants a part of it. The justification will be simple with millions upon millions of miles logged at a much safer level than human drivers. Convincing people that we should take them out of the loop will be easy.

It will start with private property large companies who have large campuses or internal transport systems. Such internal transport systems will soon be replaced them with mass transport systems that are designed to work a predictable route at nonlethal speeds. These technologies in simple form are starting to appear like the new driverless pods at Heathrow airport which allow four people to be commuted between the airport and the parking lot.[29]

Unfortunately, once this starts to be applied to public transport and logistics, and it will, a whole host of jobs is going to disappear almost overnight.

Your average taxi driver is going to find that this technology can outcompete him at a much lower cost. Consumers will enjoy the extra room and the luxury experience of being in a cab that just picks them up and drops them off. The only aspect humans can control is the destination. There will always be technophobes that will never get into a self-driving car, but ultimately it will be a quick transition because of the compelling economical advantages. A self-driving electric car will have almost no running costs beyond the initial capital outlaid. Imagine paying a dollar for a ride that is safer and more comfortable than spending ten dollars for a random stranger to pick you up.

But, that is only the tip of the iceberg. Things really start changing when logistics companies jump on the bandwagon. There are 1.25m commercial vehicles on the roads and the number is growing.[30] They make sure our supermarkets are full of groceries, that our *Amazon* orders arrive on our doorsteps, and form the backbone of transportation for most commercial activities. It's also very expensive; each human behind the wheel of a truck can cost over $55,000 a year.[31] The average lifespan of a truck is 10 years. Cutting out more than half a million dollars of operational cost per truck is a game changer in logistics. It may create a new logistics giant to compete with *DHL* or *FedEx* on this scale, but perhaps these companies will be able to adopt the new technology quickly enough to keep up with the competition. This will probably be the last nail in the coffin for the United States Postal Service, your friendly mailman will absolutely be replaced by private companies operating robotic trucks. All these jobs are going to disappear its just a matter of time.

But, how will these self-driving trucks deliver goods? It is one thing to drive to a house and quite another to select the parcel and then knock on the door and deliver the package. This is where the convergence of technology, not just robotics, becomes really powerful, and why robotics should never be evaluated in isolation to the rest of the technological spectrum. The robotic trucks of the future will be able to come and find you even if you are on the move away from home. Then, biometric identification will allow you to access an onboard "locker" and retrieve your goods.

While self-driving vehicles will revolutionize our road networks, their effects will be felt even further when mass transport systems start to feel the effect of everyone having their own personal chauffeur driven car that can drive hundreds of miles or further on a single charge. As this opens up new business models, such as on demand hire, the cost per mile per passenger will plummet to levels where mass transport systems' primary benefits of low cost and speed become eroded. The technology exists today to equip an electric car with a self-drive capability from San Francisco to Los Angeles at one hundred and ninety miles per hour.[32] This trip will span a little over two hours and cost around two dollars of electricity. (I am extrapolating a little here. Faster speeds lead to lower efficiencies, therefore shortened range and higher energy costs.) However, at the same time, technology is improving and reducing in cost, so it is likely to exceed these numbers in the near future anyway.

The economics look great even if you take into account the capital cost of the technology. Let's say this electric car can hold four people and it is at 50% capacity on average. Let's say a next generation rental company buys the car for $100,000. The car travels back and forth four times a day with just two people in the car each time, for 365 days a year. That is almost three thousand people a year served by that car, and the car will probably last for three years with a pessimistic resale value of $20,000. That would mean that the depreciation cost per passenger over 3 years would be around $9 plus, let's say, an energy cost of $2, or $11 in total. Let's say the rental company wants to make a 100% markup to cover maintenance, infrastructure, insurance, and profit etc. That puts the price of a ticket from San Francisco to Los Angeles at around $22.

To put this into context, the new high-speed rail link that is costing the US taxpayer upwards of $65 billion dollars and won't be finished until 2028.[33] The proposed system will be slower, it will not take you door to door, and have an average ticket price of around $50. That's more than 200% more expensive than the cost of a private trip using a self-driving electric car. This, of course, would require dedicated high-speed self-driving motorway lanes and some other infrastructure, but the cost would be a fraction of the equivalent infrastructure for trains. This should have the same disruptive effect on the bus industry as well, so if you were planning to get a job in mass transportation, the odds could be stacked against you.

This could even start to erode the airline industry on short-range flights if the economics and convenience factor becomes so overwhelming that for short trips you can go door to door in the comfort of your own car at half the speed of air-travel. This is not even taking into account the two to three hours we waste on our way to and in the airport. It also eliminates the possibility of a TSA giving you a rubdown with a latex glove!

It may sound absurd to suggest that air travel itself will implement the automated driver treatment, as even I would have to swallow hard before boarding a pilotless plane. Yet the pilotless plane is already flying through our skies, having completed its first automated test flight.[34] Those of you who are afraid of flying may be appalled at such a concept, but as with driving, you are more likely to die from human error than mechanical error while in the air.[35]

The pressure to keep pilots in the loop will prevail for a long time on passenger jets. But, as the economic benefits become more obvious, I am sure a progressive airline like Virgin will offer $10 fares for the first who entrust their lives to electrons. Anyway, can you imagine the view you would get at the front of the plane if they removed the cabin?

Pilotless cockpits will first appear in air cargo planes, where the phycology of the passengers(boxes) does not need to be taken into consideration. Then, maybe it will revolutionize the private jet market. However, don't think for a minute that a human will not be in the ultimate loop. As soon as a plane encounters the smallest of unpredictable behaviors, such as a sub system failure, it will switch to command and a human will provide backup control.

Although, the desire to keep human input always in the loop could be one of this technology's big unknown risks. As we cover in the next chapter, it only takes a good hacker at a computer to recreate the tragedy of September the 11th from the comfort of their sofa.

# CHAPTER 5: POLICE, MILITARY AND THE RISE OF THE MACHINES

When most people think about robots and guns, the first imagery that comes to mind is the *Terminator*. The thought that robots could be designed to kill humans is deeply disturbing. However, robots are killing humans in every major military conflict. Robotic murder of human life is being explored in almost every military research and development center around the world, as the robotic militarization of our armies, navies and air forces become a reality.

The concept of arming robots is almost as old as the concept of robots themselves. The Russian army invented *Teletanks*, which were robotic tanks controlled over a wire. *Teletanks* had some serious flaws, but it instigated an accelerated arms race over the last five decades.[36]

The first time we saw robotics in a police or military setting was for the disposal of bombs; a whole host of specialist machines were created to diffuse bombs from a distance, but these really were no more than fancy remote controlled robots with cameras. These bomb diffusing robots were the first robots to really save lives. A robot could be blown up at great expense, but it was nothing compared to the value of a human life.

However, robot manufactures realized that if one could save human lives by using robot technology, one could also apply the same strategies to killing human enemies. Even though there is something deeply unsettling about a robot being able to kill a human, we have an extremely common precedent by which to judge it. Every time a self-guided missile is launched, it uses the same basic principles that are used when robots kill. You simply set the target and launch. With a robot, in a similar fashion, you set the target (the enemy) and engage. Currently, humans are always kept in the loop; they always pull the trigger to engage the enemy.

But, this occurs when humans are in the loop. We are starting to reach the point in military robotics in which the technology itself determines whether to kill or not, or as I refer to as the "math of death." After all, all a robot is capable of is taking in a set of data, processing it, and making a probability calculation. If you are on the right side of the calculation, you live, and if you're on the wrong side, you die. Then again, if we must go that route, we must consider what would happen if there was a glitch or error of some form in the system. A glitch would most likely occur at a small percentage of any given combat engagements and perhaps cost a fraction of the lives compared to human error. But, does that make it worth the risk? That glitch could also somehow messes up the robot's calculation logic, causing it to attack the people it is supposed to protect. Now, who said that math wasn't important?

Robotics is already changing the face of warfare. You only have to take a look at the rise of unmanned aerial vehicles (UAV), or, as they're more commonly known, drones, to realize that the future of robotic warfare is already upon us. The rapid development of UAVs has been unprecedented and quickly evolving. The benefits of UAVs are undeniable; they started off just as eyes in the sky that allowed spying on unsuspecting enemies for extended periods of time, but soon developed into more complex forms, paralleling the chronological pattern of all other robotics. UAVs can now sport a whole host of complicated weaponry, land and take off from extremely short runways, and will soon be able to take off vertically or stay airborne indefinitely through the use of solar energy and batteries. Quite simply, UAVs are an air force pilot's worse nightmare when it comes to their jobs. That's not to say flying UAVs is unskilled in any way. Some may imagine flying UAVs to be like a video game, but if you had millions of dollars worth of equipment sitting at your fingertips, you would understand the commitment and skill these UAV pilots need to have. Now, the reason why a traditional pilot's job is on the line is due to excess capacity. You see, to keep the USA military as powerful as it is, different scenarios around the world are predicted with a finite number of humans on hand to fight, fly or sail to the rescue of any conflict. The military plans for a constant excess capacity in the system, i.e. enough extra people to cover most eventualities. Currently, the air force needs to calculate the physical presence of these pilots to make these calculations. In order to have the ability to deploy one hundred combat-ready pilots across two war theaters, (fancy military name for conflict zone) you need closer to three hundred pilots, as you need to account for everything from time zones, equipment availability, maintenance, to accommodation and fatigue and, most importantly, potential casualties.

But, the equation changes greatly when you have a central point of control and command. Firstly, you consider massive scales of efficiency. A single UAV pilot can theoretically control UAVs across multiple war theaters (even though for practical purposes they would normally be limited to one war theater for continuity unless there was a serious strain on resources). A UAV pilot can hop from one UAV to another instantly while it is being refueled or is destroyed. The only limitation is fatigue, which would be less than your average pilot due to the stress reduction of being out of a conflict zone, as well as a more controlled environment. So, rather than needing three hundred pilots for two war theaters, you need closer to one hundred and fifty pilots to achieve the same combat capability, or a loss of 50% of the required jobs to achieve the same. This is also before UAVs achieve the capability to make decisions themselves.

It is unlikely, however, that the military would remove pilots from the equation in the near future. For one, remotely controlled UAVs and other remote controlled military technology suffer from one big Achilles' heel, which is that any wireless communication technology is both subject to interruption, substitution or hacking. You see, for all of our miraculous technology, the physics of wireless communication is not kind. You only have to walk around with your cell phone in a low signal area to see how fragile wireless communications can be. "But the military is far more sophisticated than cell phone technology," I hear you say. Well, yes it is, but not by much. They have stronger, more redundant, and certainly more secure technology. However, it still suffers from the basic problems of radio communication. At a very basic level, there is a very low level of energy in radio signals that can be interrupted easily. This is what is thought to have happened when Iran managed to land an American UAV that was spying on them. It is believed that they simply spoofed the very weak GPS signal the UAV was receiving with a much stronger ground signal. The UAV locked onto the new GPS signal of the Iranians, so the UAV thought it was in a different position and at a different height. At the same time, the Iranians most likely overwhelmed the main radio frequency that the military used to communicate with the UAV, so that the drone was effectively flying blind and would have gone into a backup mode.

Why is this relevant when we are talking about military jobs? This scenario indicates that it tactically makes more sense for the military to start building autonomous UAVs and robots, devices that can make their own decisions based upon situational awareness. The US military is already concentrating on this development, the DARPA grand challenge competition gives a two million dollar prize to any robotic team that can drive across the desert and perform a number of tasks autonomously[37]. This is what the military ultimately desires; we make the decisions on who, what, when and where, but the technology will begin to decide how. Once we reach this point, the only jobs required will be that of the decision makers, strategists and, of course, the maintenance and deployment teams for the technology. That is, of course, until the point in which they become replaced by robots themselves.

However, this is not all bad. After all, it will save countless human lives, and allow the western developed worlds to maintain military security without the huge costs in personnel and GDP. But, it also means that the estimated 3.8 million jobs that the military in the United States directly or indirectly support will decrease in favor for more targeted, high skilled decision making, research and development building and, of course, further robotics development.[38]

Will the soldier of the future look like the *Terminator* or something else? Well, there is no doubt that humanoid functioning military robots will be developed. A quick look at *Boston Dynamics* new robots will show you how close we are to creating humanoid fighters. However, there is a good chance that some of the most effective military robotic technology will rely on *swarm technology.*[39] Instead of one very expensive robot that costs hundreds of thousands of dollars and can be damaged by a well positioned rocket launcher or grenade, *swarm technology* implements flying swarm bots that will cost hundreds of dollars. The swarm bots will communicate with each other, and overwhelm almost any attack from earth, sea or air. The enemy will have thousands of targets which will seek out human life signatures, a bit like a heat-seeking missile. Once a few of these drop next to the target, the onboard camera will transmit a picture of the human target and surrounding environment to command. Those humans in "command" will determine whether or not the drone will explode based on the transmitted image. Perhaps, these robots will be able to prevent the more lethal effects of an incoming weapon or impending attack by arranging themselves into a protective grid, thus sacrificing themselves and self-detonating much like mines do. This, in turn, will detonate the enemy weapon, and in the process will save not only valuable infrastructure, but even more valuable soldiers and military personnel. Want to bring down a jet for $500 rather than fire a $500,000 missile? It's simple. Simply fly these swarm bots in a net formation so that they will become the ultimate air mines that will move in unison towards the target. Don't think that these swarm bots will run out of batteries; there will always be extra swarm bots charging in rotation to maintain the net. Those of you who are geeky enough to watch *Star Trek Voyager* may remember a similar technology in the 46th episode.[40]

This technology of swarm bots is not hundreds of years away. In fact, most of it has been developed for search and rescue already.[41] However, swarm technology will not be limited to offense or defense. It will change the nature of everything from logistics to building bases. One of the technologies that I am working on at the moment is a self-building fence that literally can crawl out of shipping containers and build a self-repairing, intelligent, monitoring fence that generates electricity from renewable energy. Bases of the future will be dropped off in shipping containers and twelve hours later will secure to fully encased bases with power on tap.

Using a robotic force against an enemy who wants to attack is one thing, but what happens when the government starts using robots to enforce laws amongst its own citizens? Well, as much as Orwell's "Big Brother" tried to teach us a lesson about the risks of CCTV and tracking technology, we still ignored it. However, Big Brother has a way of creeping up on us. In order to function normally in our society, we have a device on us 24 hours a day that can be tracked and interrogated to disclose all of our secrets. It can even allow technology to predict our movements.[42] Yet, we put up with this fact without worrying too much because we have the illusion that it is our choice to carry a phone or be in an area with CCTV. Only now, that is no longer a choice. We live in a world in which you always have to be connected. It is very hard, if not impossible, to function in normal society without this technology, and it is as useful as the monetary device known as cash. A great deal of people complain about how technology invades our privacy, but there is always a cost to living in a society. Ultimately, if you wanted, you could go and live in a forest, kill animals and build shelter in order to survive as a human in complete privacy. We choose not to do this because the benefits of our society outweigh the negatives. Thus, privacy is ultimately dead and it is going to become much worse.

It is without a doubt that law enforcement will start to use robotic technology more and more. The use of drones for police work is slowly being implemented, but it is unlikely that one will see Robocop sentries any time soon. [43] Initially, security robots will start to infiltrate the private security sector.

Dogs and people roaming around buildings and warehouses is expensive, inefficient and prone to human failure.[44] A couple of infrared flying drones controlled by a central command post is very efficient and reliable, and most importantly, is massively lower in cost. Most sectors will utilize robots in conjunction with command and control centers operated by a few humans. However, this action will replace tens of thousands of jobs rapidly. It's basic economics that the first company to efficiently produce automated robotic security will be able to dominate the industry. That is, until the rest of the security industry catches up, and it will have to do so quickly.

Combining robots with biometrics systems will remove another entire layer of employment, as building entries are secured by automated biometric systems that will be able to pull almost any data using face recognition. Biometrics will allow entry into low-level security buildings, such as offices. Anomalies will be dealt with through a central command structure run by humans. However, the reality is that humans are really quite inefficient at detecting suspicious activities, even when it is their job to do so.[45]

So, will police robots ever roam the streets Robocop style? Even though it is likely that robots will replace private security, I doubt that it will replace policing activities fully. I don't think that citizens would allow that kind of decision making to happen autonomously. Secondly, crime by its very nature is relatively unpredictable, as in high stress situations, humans become irrational. Judging this irrationality will be very difficult for technology. However, I do think that a number of specialist robots will be developed to work alongside police, much like the military use of drones and surveillance bots. We are even witnessing movement towards the use robots for the purposes of interrogation. Sounds crazy, right? Police are highly trained to force the truth out of people, but people may change the truth in their minds, depending on which questions they are asked and how they are asked them. It has been shown that, actually, an independent robot asking questions and interacting with a witness could be a much safer way of interrogation. The participants are also less likely to create fictitious statements.[46]

Those who are unlucky to find themselves in prison will also find themselves surrounded by robots. South Korean correctional facilities are already implementing them, and given the relatively predictable nature of a prison environment, robots are the perfect prison guards.[47] They will be incorruptible all-seeing, all-hearing guards that will be able to detect unusual behavior patterns and warn beforehand of any likely security problems. It is also likely that they will be able to monitor and track contraband in a way that humans cannot through some simple additional sensors and electronic devices. Robot guards will even have the ability to see through inmates' clothes. Such guards will also help remove the need for suicide watch or solitary confinement, as a robot guard can be assigned to a specific prisoner.

But ultimately, robots would free the high number of incarcerated people by allowing for much more invasive probation monitoring through the use of robotic technology. In such cases, robots that follow and shadow the prisoner in exchange for his or her freedom may be a trade that most incarcerated felons are willing to make. The cost benefits would be outstanding, given the $74 billion+ a year the USA spends on incarceration. In exchange, prison guards and parole officers may become a dying species. But, I am sure that the incarcerated will not be too sad about that. [48]

Since this is a chapter on law enforcement, it might be important to consider the possibilities of an entire overhaul of the justice system. Now, I'm not saying that you'd be having robots complete your jury duty for you, or represent you in a court of law (although, why not?). Research is already being conducted regarding turning laws into computer code, so that computers can start to decide the merits of such cases.[49] Perhaps, specialized robots could act as notaries, which would only be accessible when both parties of an agreement are present, have had their biometric identities confirmed, and have voiced their agreement of their said contract. Signatures could and should become consigned to history. On the other hand, what about infusing the present technology available of lie detection, albeit much more sophisticated, available during questioning in a court room? Now, let us venture into the possibility of robotic lawyers, or robotic jurors or even robotic judges. The concept, at the present, seems very abstract. We could get to a stage where robots become our judge. Robotic juries and executioners have shown impartiality and fairness beyond our human peers. But, just as an exercise for your imagination, consider it. Additionally, let's go a step further into our legislative representatives. If the future is one where everyone is connected, then why not have people directly vote on bills, on reforms and on existing laws?

This micro-democracy would be the truest sense of democracy and could cut the possibilities of corruption and lobbying. The technology already exists to make this happen. In the past, we needed our representatives to do the voting for us because of the vast distance from our homes to the nation's capital. But now, with the internet, it's very possible for most of our population, if not the entire nation, to be able to access these bills, give their vote and move on. This would bring the power of the vote and legislation rightly so into the hands of citizens. Then again, such a structure is perceptible to hackers and the like, and thus one could argue that such a possibility could undermine democracy. Until we can safeguard our cyberspace completely, I suppose, senators and representatives will still have their jobs. So, congressmen nationwide, rest easy!

Now consider this: will robots put drug dealers and murderers out of a job? If there was ever a perfect application for a robot, it would be in the world of crime. It's a Hollywood favorite for films, and it is obvious that this is one area in which humans and robots could start being at odds with each other.

The ability to carry our physical crimes remotely will be incredibly alluring to the criminal world. We already see it today with credit card theft, which is a $20 billion a year industry.[50] In a certain respect, I am surprised that it has not been taken advantage of sooner since even the basic technology we have today could easily be adapted for criminal enterprises.

The first crimes we will see will be related to the drug industry. Already, there are UAV drug mules.[51] It would not surprise me if there are continual automated submarines darting back and forth from Colombia to the USA.[52] But, this is just the beginning. The drug business is simply a combination of some of the technologies I have already discussed. Drugs will be grown by farm bots. They will be transported by UAVs, cut by manufacturing bots and distributed by self-driving cars.

This, combined with the sex trade having to deal with the introduction of sex bots, will likely cause the estimated $2 trillion shadow economy to take a hit in employment.[53] One doesn't have to look too far to see how many people are employed by the shadow economy. Robotics will replace large parts of the shadow economy as the benefit of low-cost unregulated markets becomes eroded by robotic technology that achieves the same outcomes.

While the drug industry will most likely be the first adopters of this robotic technology, it will be fascinating to see the creativity of crimes that humans will make robots commit. It will probably span the whole spectrum of criminal activities, from a group of bored kids reprogramming a painting bot to create graffiti to someone reprogramming it to commit a murder.

Robotic murders will be easy to achieve and easy to get away with. After all, robots are the perfect criminals. They do not leave any evidence, they carry out the crime perfectly, and then can be destroyed at the moment of success. While you might be picturing a humanoid robot holding a gun, it is much more likely that such technology will be an automated sniper gun that picks the targeted victim off at a moment's notice.[54] Whether or not this technique will start to be used by governments to kill high profile targets without leaving any evidence will be the ultimate test of robotics in the world of law enforcement. After all, the device can be placed in a strategic position weeks before an event and remotely controlled on the day to implement the perfect murder. As I discussed regarding the nature of drones, and "evolutionary" chip-powered robots, your friendly helper robots could be reprogrammed for murder given the right hack and commands, or could perhaps even be corrupted on their own to commit crimes. Could a helper robot pick up a knife and stab somebody? It is feasible. Even if manufacturers do implement the *Three Laws of Robotics*, the laws are still simply rules written in code that can be modified.[55] If mankind can be corrupted not to follow laws, how can we be so sure that robots, who are in a sense the creative offspring of mankind, will be programmed such that they would be incorruptible? Again, the possibilities of glitches, as well as some shady hacker, to reprogram a robot's "mind" are always there.

However, there are technologies we can implement to protect ourselves, to some degree, from the anonymous nature of technology. Obviously, every robot will have its own unique identifier, and its core programming may be built in ROM so that it cannot be modified without a replacement chip. But, if cyber warfare has taught us anything, it's that the criminals almost always find a way to get around these protections.

# CHAPTER 6: AGRICULTURE, MINING AND WHEN BOTS GET DIRTY

Farming bots are one of the very few industries in which robots will be critical to humanity's survival and quality of life. Think about it. Humanity's necessities and its entire basis for life and leaps and bounds in evolution, arguably, is linked to agriculture. Because of agriculture, mankind began to settle in locations, and from those settlements created such civilizations as those of Ancient Egypt, Ancient Babylonia, and the Indus Valley civilization. Due to the basis of agriculture, many great civilizations brought up culture, grand architecture, religion and mythos that historically cultivated societies which grew into our own sense of the present. Instead of spending time hunting and gathering, humanity now found a way to calculate the seasons and create sciences around it, such as astronomy. We depended upon those seasons to sustain our lives. This new knowledge allowed us to store extra food, and still provided us time to pursue our creativity and expand the populace at exponential rates.

Due to present climate change, water shortages and population growth, humanity now cannot sustain the number of mouths it has to feed worldwide. We have already seen the early effects of this on the planet. It's nice and idealistic to think of the Arab Spring Revolutions in 2010 as humanity's beautiful revolution of overthrowing evil dictators. However, the reality is that the revolution was primarily driven by the crop failures in the previous years, which pushed up the price of staple foods for poor populations by up to 40%.[56] As the climate continues to change, we are more likely to see massive crop failures that will start increasing food prices and cause political and social instability. As with most of humanity's problems, ironically, those who are least able to adapt will be the first to suffer.

It is theorized that the reason humans developed much bigger brains than our primate equivalent was because we discovered fire for light, heat and cooking. Through cooking, we could obtain many more calories from our food than by eating it raw.[57] This was the start of our agriculture revolution, which allowed us to continue feeding more mouths with greater efficiency. But as with a great deal of technology, once it matures it begins a process of diminishing returns. It is designed to squeeze more and more out of less and less, which has resulted in our current agricultural crisis. It's high time that we need another agricultural revolution with technology in its mix to feed the masses.

Some claim that one of the reasons why we have been able to continually sustain our growth in agriculture is due to the energy we gain from oil. A single barrel of oil is said to be equivalent in energy of a human working a field for twelve years.[58] No wonder we have managed to keep our quality of life stable while our population has boomed.

This revolution won't just come from robotics. Genetically modified crops and artificial farming will play an integral part in increasing efficiency. At some point, we will have the ability to "print" our food using In Vitro or test tube food.[59] It's not as far away as you might think.

In the near future, robotics will have a massive impact on farming. A field is a much more controllable environment than a road network. Thus, self-driving tractors that can tend to massive amounts of land 24 hours a day are already being developed.[60] Initially, this will help farmers efficiently plow their land without tractor drivers. Except for the tractor drivers, the placement of self-driving tractors will not really reduce farm labor that much. That process already occurred hundreds of years ago when thousands of laborers were replaced by rudimentary farm technology such as the plough. In fact, if you want to see how technology has an impact on jobs, simply look at the graph on the next page that demonstrates how technology obliterated farming jobs over the last one hundred and fifty years. Technology's impact on industry did not fair much better as again you will see from the graph.

Even if you own a farm with one hundred tractors, the most you are going to do with self-driving tractors is replace one hundred jobs and increase efficiency by allowing 24 hour farming to take place.

However, there is still a vast amount of casual farm labor that requires the dexterity and senses of humans to perform it. Generally, such labor entails picking-related jobs that do not exactly consist of easily replicable tasks.

Even livestock management will be performed via robotic control. The robotic sheep dog was worked on in the 1990's by Oxford University, and it is only a matter of time before these niche commercial robots begin to appear.[61]

So what does a farm look like in the future? It is probably not far off from a centralized security office. We will almost certainly keep a human in the farming loop for a long period of time, if only for our own illusion of control. I can also imagine the insurance companies requiring it for liability purposes; if a

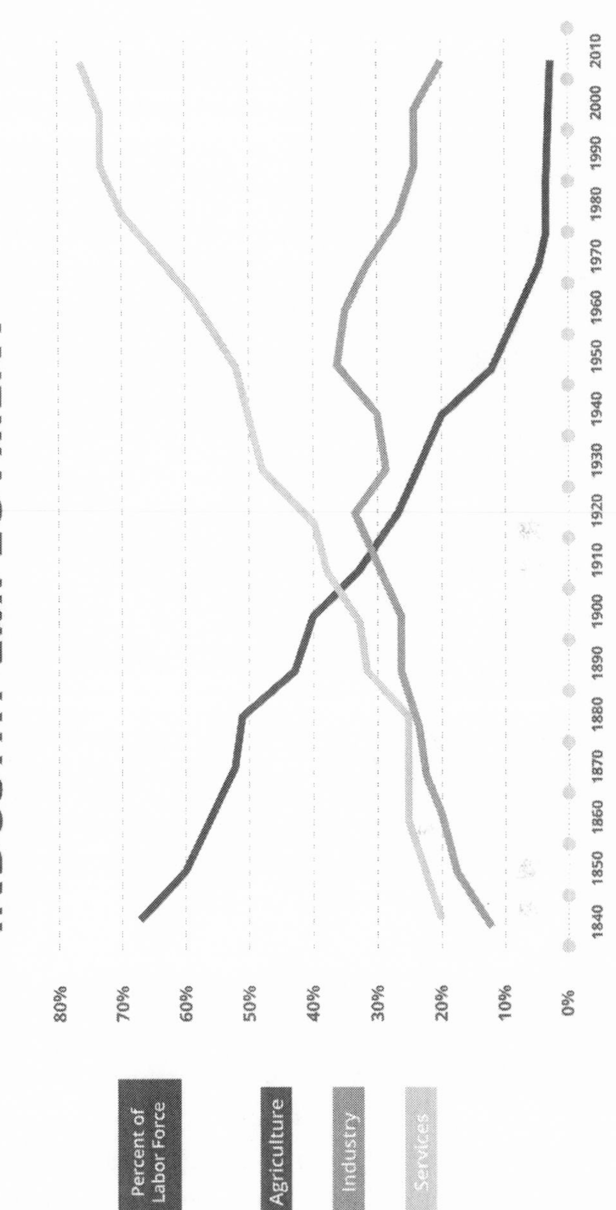
DECLINE IN AGRICULTURE
AND
INDUSTRY EMPLOYMENT
Percent of Labor Force
Agriculture
Industry
Services
80%
70%
60%
50%
40%
30%
20%
10%
0%
1840
1850
1860
1870
1880
1890
1900
1910
1920
1930
1940
1950
1960
1970
1980
1990
2000
2010
Decade

robotic combine harvester runs over a couple making love in a field, then somebody has to be responsible, right? Well, the fact remains that it is highly unlikely that a robotic harvester would run over two humans, given its audio and infrared sensors. Additionally, the farm flying security bots would have picked the human obstacles out before harvesting ever began. Extended sensing capabilities both within the equipment and on the farm, combined with far superior climate models, will allow a much more accurate and controlled growing environment. This will allow far less resources, such as water and fertilizer, to be used or even distributed at the individual plant level for both optimal growing and resource management.

In order to increase efficiencies, farms themselves will most likely expand following a trend towards larger land management. This, in turn, will allow for a more controllable environment in which predictable terrain will enable any inconsistencies to show up immediately. Fences will disappear from within farm boundaries and around fields. After all, robots only need a line drawn on a map to understand boundaries in micro-precision. Fences around farms will most likely become far more defensive, given the desire to keep a controlled environment and increase the value of the equipment on the farm. There is also the added safety of swarming security drones.

Initially, humans will be required to provide interim processes that require transformation from one process to another. For example, a self-driven tractor with a seed planting extension will easily plant a billion seeds without hassle, but it won't be able to perform the process of taking the seeds from the supplier or emptying out the bags into a standardized seed bin so that the seed planting tractor can plant them. Taking delivery itself is a complex process, and thus this will likely remain manual until much more flexible humanoid ability robots become available that can perform a number of the simple but diverse tasks. These issues will be similar to the issues that factories and industries will face before being fully automated.

Perhaps the solution for this particular problem of diverse tasks is for industries to standardize material delivery in the same way the air cargo industry has (and to a slightly lesser extent, the sea cargo industry) so that delivery of materials is always standardized. A robotic truck would 'dock' with a farm, offload its full containers and pick up its empty ones. This would be the most efficient way to handle the process, but would also require the maximum amount of collaboration between industry partners and those managing new infrastructure work at the farms and industrial facilities. For this reason, I can't predict which is more likely to come first: a robotic technology that allows a great number of diverse tasks to be preformed efficiently, or standardization across the logistics and supplier delivery network.

It will also be interesting to see how animal welfare organizations deal with the fact that robots will be killing animals. Presently, the killing of animals is obviously mechanical, but it is a human that flicks the "on" switch. With the present shift in attitudes towards inhuman killing of animals by humans themselves, it would be quite the moral conundrum and perhaps another step in ethical revolutions, when and if the psychology of killing changes when it's at the "hands" of a robot.

Farming does not represent the only controllable environment for robots on land, and presently there are hundreds of thousands of automated devices scattered all over the country in the form of oil wells. These work bots of the oil industry go about their work year after year pulling black gold from the earth.

Thus, it won't be long before the mining industry starts using robot technology. Mine exploring robots have already been developed to safely map abandoned mines. However, mining also has its unique challenges for robots. Mine environments are quite challenging for any mechanical device, especially robotics. They are wet, dirty and can be salty; all of which are red flags for robot technology. One only has to look at the *Mars Rover* to see the innovation that was required to protect it against the harsh Martian environment.[62]

However, a great deal of these challenges will be resolved. New materials are being created and innovation in superhydrophobic water repelling technology will be able to protect robots against a lot of the moisture and water damage they would otherwise be exposed to.[63]

It is also a possibility that huge self-driving mining vehicles will become commonplace. Swarms of thousands of smaller mining bots will work together, slowly but surely breaking down the mining material, while carrier bots will collect and process the material. By using low cost micro bots that are only designed to grind and recharge constantly 24 hours a day, a mining operation could continue indefinitely, even when the micro bots fail and need to be replaced or repaired.

The same type of swarm mining bots could be used for building tunnels. Simply lay down a few thousand of these bots at either end of a tunnel, and they will grind away while communicating their positions with each other to form the perfect tunnel and meet in the middle with ease. After swarm mining bots have completed this task, concrete spraying robots will shore up the tunnel.

Because of the reduction in safety requirements (nobody cares if a few bots are crushed by falling rock), the cost of tunneling will reduce dramatically. In the U.S., it currently costs $100 million to $1 billion a mile to build a tunnel.[64] Thus, the economic incentives to build this technology are huge.

Fishing is also an area that could become highly automated. The sea, in some respects, is far more of a controllable environment than that on land. Autopilots have been used on boats for over fifty years.[65] Modern luxury cruises are already fly-by-wire machines with highly advanced automated sensors. If such a system had been activated in the past, the thirty people that lost their lives on the Costa Concordia would be alive today. With such a controllable environment, it makes sense for fishing to achieve the same overhaul as the car industry will with self driving capabilities. I suspect that the Japanese will develop fishing robotics first. However, hopefully our development of sustainable automated fish farms will come before automated fishing so that we can sustain the dwindling fish stocks.[66] Despite the availability of fish, robotic fishing boats will be able to trawl until the seas are empty.

# CHAPTER 7: EDUCATION AND THE BABY BOTS

Arguably, a parent's worst nightmare is the nanny bot. Can you think of anything worse than a robot looking after your child, nurturing it and educating it? If so, then that's probably because you're an amazing parent or were brought up by amazing parents. Unfortunately, the rest of us are not always so lucky.

The vast majority of humans are brought up in environments that are far from ideal. 26% of children in the USA are brought up in single parent homes, and while I can personally attest that this within itself is not necessarily a bad thing, almost always some kind of compromise has to be made in this environment .[67] Additionally, over half a million children are neglected per year, and for these children, robots will become as important and as loved as *Mary Poppins* .[68]

It's not like technology and robots don't already infiltrate our young children. Anyone who has seen a one year old child fascinated with an *iPad* will know that kids have an innate fascination with technology.[69] Robotics will be an extension of that, but on steroids. On that note, one might even consider that we are evolving in step with the new technology of every new generation. It's funny how babies, especially, begin to develop an inherent interest in new forms of technology, and later on toddlers and children are able to work on computers and tablets intuitively, as if the knowledge of using such technology was hardwired into their brains. Perhaps this knowledge is passed on genetically through the so called "junk" portion of our DNA.

After all, it makes sense that biological entities would pass on some basic information to help them evolve.[70] Of course, one can go further into this research, but I digress.

The robotic teddy bear is only a few years from being sold in the market, and while these initial devices will be entertaining in nature, as they develop they will have a more influential role in our children's development.[71] After all, there are very few parents who are not guilty of plopping their children in front of the TV for extended amounts of time so they can get some well deserved rest. The robotic teddy will just be an extension of this, but what an extension it will be!

Apart from the occasional replaced positions of the nanny and au pair, the robotic bear is not going to destroy too many jobs. Kids will still need interaction like preschool and play groups, and while some may imagine these being run by robots, it is unlikely that robots would replace humans in these environments, as psychologically it will be hard for humans to leave our helpless young children entirely at the hands of robotic helpers. However, they will surely make their way into these environments, either replacing assistants or providing parents a remote way to interact with their children. Who would not want to see and interact with their children while they are hard at work? The perfect distraction during that long day at work is to be spending time with the children you love.

When children get older and less helpless, the psychological restrictions will start to disappear. With the realities of life, parents will want to educate and care for their children in the most economical way they can.

The first set of education bots will most likely be very specific and niche in nature, rather than try and be all things to all people. Companies will find specific areas where robots excel in a controlled environment. Want to learn how to play the piano? Simple. Just sit next to the piano bot, watch and copy with feedback and encouragement from your automated friend. The economic and social benefits for a parent are huge; not only can they rent it (brought to you on that night by an automated robotic service), but it will sit there with your son and daughter until they have done as little or as much as they can, rather than trying to fit everything into an abstract hour. The children are supervised by a safe, responsible, nonthreatening robot (I'm not suggesting that piano teachers are creepy, but mine was!) while automatically adjusting to your children's skills and abilities. How many skilled musicians have we lost due to teachers enforcing their view on how music should be played? I am not even suggesting that robotic tutors need necessarily be as good as their human counterparts, only that the economics allow far more children to experience the subject. The piano is just one example, and as robots become more and more sophisticated, they will be able to perform more and more of these roles. This is a real shame, as a lot of niche art experts and tutors will lose positions to robots. While robots will never be able to replicate the experience of a tutor or the passion of an expert, they will ultimately open these niche subjects up to much a wider and diverse set of students that would not otherwise be able to afford it. Overall, it would be beneficial to society as a whole.

Presently, education is in a state of transition with the technologies we already have. Online schools, classes and MOOCs, massive open online courses, are becoming more and more common place. It is always a fine balance between lowering the cost of education and maintaining the quality of education that is available to everyone. The economics of education is a very expensive process that does not benefit the economy as quickly as humanity's short-sightedness would like us see. Also, age group constrained education has its massive flaws, as I will attest to personally. The classroom can only move as fast as the slowest individual(and yes, for a few classes I was that kid!) which has two undesired effects.[72] The first is being that the most intelligent kids don't learn as fast as they could and become bored, which is normally followed by disruptive behavior, and the slowest kids become frustrated and believe that they will not succeed in that subject.

However, sticking kids in front of computers at home to educate themselves is also not the answer. One of the massive benefits of school is not the education itself, but the social development that comes with being with multiple age groups and individuals. I imagine an educational environment which is much more fluid, more like today's co-working spaces in which common spaces give way to specialist learning areas, where children can ask teachers in a nonthreatening environment about what they are learning or allow them to use equipment they need in order to educate themselves in that subject. The age groups will be much more interactive and diverse, fostering a school family and community. While I still believe that human specialist teachers will continue to play a role, a great deal of the ancillary positions will become irrelevant. Interactive robots will be able to provide focus points for education, and even allow the student to be connected directly with specialist teachers from across the world. This will allow specialization into subject fields at a much earlier age. Individual content acquisition is currently being explored in the "flipped classroom model", in which students learn objective content individually, often with the aid of a computer, while teacher led class time is used for building critical thinking skills, discussion and collaborative projects with classmates. Class time, in turn, builds the creative and social skills that a robot may not be able to foster in a student.

Information and knowledge will be ubiquitous, as much of it already is with the facts of text books readily available through the internet. Through MOOCs, international students that did not have access to an ivy league education can now sit in on lectures from Stanford and UC Berkeley professors. This, of course, is not the same as sitting with a professor in a small seminar style graduate or undergraduate classroom, but MOOCs do provide a lens into the ivy league campus that would not otherwise be possible for many students.

In the future,, if you want a job, you will need to become a super specialist if you do not plan to work in the creative industries. If technology can answer 95% of today's knowledge requirements in a particular job, then you must know damn well how to do that other 5%.

We have already seen how technology has destroyed a huge number of education jobs. You may not have even realized it. This is because a great deal of these education positions are in the private sector, and because they are not considered "teachers" in the traditional sense, we don't see them in the same way. Think twenty years ago how many people were sent on health and safety course, sexual harassment courses and the like? Cringe worthy as they were, you would be educated in the requirements of that field, take a test, have it marked and hopefully show your boss the pass slip. Even with today's limited technology, we have destroyed almost all of these jobs with a simple online education course, and this is just the start of the process.

Higher education is likely to suffer the most rapidly.[73] Indeed there is already uproar in the quality and verifiability of online courses and the effect on the finances of higher education departments.[74] I suspect at the moment you have a vision of a clunky robot at the front of a lecture hall flailing its arms about. Our tendency to humanize robots and place them in familiar situations is why robotics always seems so farfetched. While at some point, it is possible that humanoid robots could perform this type of interaction, it is unlikely that they will, as the information they contain will be so ubiquitous online that it becomes inefficient for them to communicate the information in that way. But, it is likely that collaborative robots will be able to work and keep an eye on students' progress much better than an individual professor ever could. I can imagine scenarios where edubots work one-on-one with students in specialist environments such as biology, and monitor, interact and help them; for those questions that the robot teacher is not equipped to deal with, quite simply the robot will connect to a remote professor who will then use telepresence (a fancy word for advanced video conferencing) to explain the solution directly. An early version of this is already starting to happen in traditional education where the flipped classroom model is gaining traction.[75]

Perhaps the greatest change in education will not come from access knowledge itself. We now have access to all the information in the world in front of us 24 hours a day. As technology becomes more intelligent, it will even start predicting what we need to learn before we know ourselves. The most valuable gift we can give our children may not be to teach them information or knowledge in traditional subjects, but to teach them the skills to learn by themselves.

# CHAPTER 8: RETAIL, DRINK AND FOOD WITH BOOZY BOTS

I hate the thought of our coffee coming from a machine. Don't you? Press a button and a little cup drops down, filled with probably the worst coffee you have ever tasted. Machines are just terrible at this seemingly simple task, but it is not their fault entirely. When we try and combine machinery with food and drink, we try and combine them in areas with extremely limited space with limited access to fresh ingredients. We also limit the options, as each new option requires a new process which requires the hardware to become more expensive and prone to breakdown. Presently, at least, it's not realistically conceivable for such machinery to be able to take your order (without the sometimes lousy customer service we sometimes face) and fulfill it with ease, precision and timeliness. As I've discussed earlier, today's modern day robots are limited to repetitive tasks.

But, we should not write off the possibility of robotics in the food and drink industry. The reality is that most food preparation can be completed in a relatively controlled environment. In fact, the most successful fast food companies have built their success on this basis. *Subway* employees, for example, may just seem to grab you a handful of pepperoni to put on your sandwich, but in fact every ingredient is controlled to a minute level. In effect, you have a human robot behind the counter of a *Subway* store. It won't be long before some entrepreneur figures out that by getting rid of staff members and replacing them with robots that don't sneeze over the food, it will reduce the cost of a sub by 20-30% and will produce a business model that is very profitable.

However, it is always the exception and not the rule that makes an environment like a *Subway* restaurant hard for robots to manage completely. Robots of the future will be able to manage this to some degree, and will improve complex skills over time. Despite this, there will always be a time in which the environment changes so much that a robot just can't perform as well as a human. Will a robot be able to cope with a situation that is beyond their programmed capabilities? Probably not for a long time. Initially, we will find robots doing the bulk of the "heavy lifting", while humans tend to execute more nuanced interactions. However, at some point, the humans will disappear from the loop. I have alluded to this idea in an earlier chapter, as telepresence will take up a lot of this slack. When a robot cannot understand or interpret a human's behavior or request, it will simply link back to a human operator. Think of when you call up your bank and hear that annoying interactive system that is so difficult to understand. You have to speak to an operator who generally sounds like he or she is based in India, and who may or may not have a comprehensible accent. Therefore, don't be surprised if a robot does not understand you and then a nice friendly Indian pops up on the screen and asks you what you would like to order. When you're placing your order and the robot does not understand (the reality is that there will not be any ambiguity in ordering, as it will all be done beforehand on your cell phone, Google glasses or brain implant!) you might find yourself staring at your Indian friend ready to clarify your order and relay that information back to the store.

I am sure that customers will initially be repulsed by the idea of robots making our food. The reality is that the technology presently exists to automate most of what *McDonald's* requires to make its meals. I am not sure if *McDonald's* is in the process of actively researching this, but they have clearly chosen to stick with human power for now. I suspect their customer research has shown that humans currently would be uncomfortable with an entirely automated process. Maybe the psychology behind this is partly to do with the fact that if the food preparation process is completely automated, then where is *McDonald's* actually adding the value? Maybe the perception is that it becomes no more valuable than a burger that you put in the microwave.

But wait until you have actually tried the robot made burger, as I have been lucky enough to experience with *Momentum Machines*, which have already developed a gourmet burger robot with mouth watering results. This completely automated process can produce four hundred gourmet burgers an hour that taste twice as good at half the price of any fast food chain.

No doubt, at some point, the economics and the value perception will change. After all, *McDonald's* is very successful in making food taste far better than it should.

Having robots in the kitchen should also open the doorway to more food customization, as opposed to less. Once the technology becomes more mature, people will be able to specify almost any theoretical combination of ingredients. Not only will this have a massive benefit for people on diets or those who have allergies, but it will also have the added advantage of setting off a million marketing opportunities for companies that increasingly realize the value of treating their customers as individuals. Do you want your Burger King Whopper well done, without tomato, with some extra lettuce, whole-wheat bun, mustard and peppers?

You got it!

As with most robotics adoption, the first time they will be utilized will be when a product or service is oversubscribed, just like when you check in now at airports and you have the choice of waiting in line or checking in through their check-in kiosk. Eventually, after you are fed up with waiting in line, you reach a critical point where you try the new technology. This experience is what drives a lot of behavior change. Simple frustration.

This frustration is evident whenever you meet an attractive girl and you offer them a drink. You only find that the bar queue is ten people deep and that you would give anything to buy this person a drink right now, rather than wait the twenty minutes to be served and your chances of keeping her attention diminish quickly.

The booze bot is definitely on its way. In fact, I have been served by one, and while some bar banter would have been nice, in a situation that demands it, robotic bartenders will become more and more commonplace.[76] We already have automated bars and the jury is still out on whether or not they will work in the wider market.[77] Initially, I think that our booze bots will be there primarily to deal with times when bartenders cannot cope with demand. Having a robot to bring you a drink may be an optional luxury, or it may be used when you can't be bothered to wait at the bar. In some senses, this is an extension of alcoholic vending machines that already exist, but with the addition of an extensive number of freshly made drinks and some pretty clever artificial intelligence banter.

These machines may be so good at their job that they will create their own demise. After all, it is rare for a barman to tell us that we have had too much to drink, but when the booze bots analyze your breath to determine how drunk you are, you could be looking at one of the most annoying robots in the world. Unlike your local barman, who you can probably convince to give you that one last drink, the booze bot's decision will be final. The one advantage, apart from the fact that the booze bot will be able to ID you instantly, is that it will not only know your favorite drink, based upon your previous orders, but it will also be able to suggest drinks that you may never have even thought about. It will provide all of these services while listening to your boring love life challenges without judgment. Eventually, the all-robotic bar will become a reality and bartender jobs will only exist in the classiest of venues who can still afford human labor.

Eventually, most transactions in the real world will not be processed by humans. We have already seen the start of this where checkouts have been replaced by self-service tills. While this is just the beginning, the whole retail experience is going to become much more automated. Before this happens, we will go through a number of stages. First off, RFID will take over from the barcode. Once this happens, the checkout process will become almost completely automated. Payment will be electronic only (cash as it stands today will only be used in the most obscure transactions, a little like how peppercorn is still used in contracts today), shelves will be stacked by robots, and security bots will roam the aisles automatically picking up suspicious behavior and running your facial features through the local crime database. Of course, there will be those who rebel against this faceless reality, but as with most things, economic necessity will make them a success.

Those of you who can't imagine what a store would look like without humans keeping check on their counterparts, you only have to look at the success of *Anytime Fitness*, an innovative health club group based in the US which operates unmanned fitness centers, a model that works. A large demographic of people are happy to pay less not to have the bells and whistles of a staff there to help them. While I am sure that they suffer their fair share of theft, the ever watchful eye of "Big Brother" is constantly watching their members' every move. It seems more than an incentive for most people not to walk off with the equipment.

I am sure that there are thousands of security guards, whose only job is to stare at a whole bunch of CCTV screens, looking for this bad behavior. However, these jobs too are in danger, as technology becomes better at understanding behavior patterns and picking up unusual events. Rather than have one security guard monitor 10 cameras, a single security guard will be able to monitor thousands simultaneously, as the technology automatically decides the images that they should be looking at. While it might be true that the technology may miss a few outlying events (which it will learn from), humans are notoriously inefficient at picking out exceptions, even when we are trained to look for them.[78]

Those who hate the thought of walking into your local supermarket will like the next development in retail even less. As we have seen, some of the most successful companies in the world *Coca Cola*, *Nike* and *Zappos* have automated their warehousing operation.[79] Well, it is only one small step to bring that to a consumer level. In a sense, we have already flirted with this model. *Best Products* in the USA and *Argos* in the UK were both catalog shops with showrooms and a warehouse in the back. In these cases, these humans were basically robots.

However, ordering from an interactive 'catalog' that knows your shopping styles and can predict what you're going to buy has limitations. One aspect retail thrives on is impulse buying. In fact, 60-70% of all grocery purchases are considered unplanned (no wonder our economy survives on consumption).[80] So, it would be hugely detrimental for sales to be moved to a completely non-retail environment. There will certainly be a transition period, and for those of you who have gone into a retail store to look at an item before purchasing it, will understand that this trend is only going to get worse for retailers. With the advent of Google glasses, people will walk around supermarkets with their augmented reality glasses, look at a product and say, 'buy.' In fact, it would not surprise me if in a few years, the sounds inside supermarkets will be echoes and whispers of "buy" "buy" "buy" like crickets in a field. If the supermarkets are clever, they will have their own fulfillment process. So, by the time you reach the end of your shopping trip, the pick and pack bots in the back will already have your produce waiting for you. However, it is far more likely that a third party company will develop this technology with automated fulfillment to your door within hours. Overall, the future will allow you to walk into almost any store, choose what you want to buy, and by the time you get home it will already be at your door, thanks to the self-driving logistics, at a fraction of the store price.

This process will just about kill retail in the way we know it today. My prediction is that eventually, we will have retail spaces that are just showrooms. Manufacturers and producers will rent shelf space and consumers will be able to browse for free while purchasing online.

You may be thinking, "Well, why do you need any retail

space at all when technology is allowing you to see every detail and experience products in minute detail before buying? Why won't people just buy online?" You only need to look at *Apple* stores to realize that there is something unique about human psychology and a human's need to touch and experience products firsthand. Even though *Apple*'s products are ubiquitous and available online, *Apple* retail spaces are among the most revenue generating spaces per square foot of any retail area.[81] Over a long period of time, this may change, especially with the development of advanced haptic devices that allow us to touch remote objects. For those of you who have not used haptic devices, they provide physical feedback in a virtual world. Haptic devices are a bit like those game controllers that vibrate when you are shot, but the new haptic devices literally allow you to run your fingers and feel surfaces as if you were there touching them; you can feel the texture, even the material. This technology will eventually reach a point in which it is indistinguishable from the real world. I still believe that the process of retail is an entertainment product for many people rather than a function. While that remains the case, I can't see retail disappearing completely. But, it will change. That change will impact a huge number of jobs. Retail provides the US with around 10% of its jobs.[82] Technology, robotics and the trend towards city migration will force retail outlets to reduce the number of stores and focus on stores covering larger geographic areas in focused retail areas. As this occurs, more and more of both the frontend and backend of retail will be replaced with automation. It is likely that the human touch will only be kept in higher end stores where a sales process is more likely to take place. These retail stores will also be helped with the self-drive revolution. I suspect that stores will start to provide free automated shuttle services for those who do not have automated cars. This, in turn, reduces the geographical constraints of retail further and provides a great opportunity for presales advertising before customers arrive at the showroom. Without the hassle or constraints of parking, sellers will be able to provide a more enjoyable experience. This will also increase the amount of retail space available as back end fulfillment will be completed off site.

# CHAPTER 9: MANUFACTURING AND WHEN ROBOTS BUILD THEMSELVES

America used to be quite good at mass production. I mean, very good. It used to be the engine that drove the economy and ensured prosperity for a generation. But, how quickly things change. By the 1970's, industry had started to feel the effects of Japanese manufacturing eating into the U.S. sector. From there, it was a challenge to compete with a worldwide trade environment which rewarded low skilled, low cost labor with little regulation, over a highly industrialized and well regulated skilled labor force. Then, of course, the beast of China took over, and for decades has monopolized the manufacturing of most products. With such a cheap labor force, there has been little incentive to invest in automation, but this is changing rapidly. Chinese manufacturing is no longer as competitive as it used to be, and for the first time in a long time, US manufacturing is starting to look attractive again. A few years ago when we manufactured, we only considered China as a possible option. However, this is changing because as China has driven huge amounts of wealth from its manufacturing and economic surge, its own living standards and economy has pushed the price of labor ever upwards. Once you take into account the logistical expenses, quality control and risks of doing business in China is really starting to look less attractive.

However, the Chinese are an industrious little bunch and they have not let this pass them by. The automation of manufacturing is rapidly developing in China. Therefore, one must wonder how it plays out in their more restricted society, as automation starts to put pressure on even very low income jobs.

The first steps towards this complete automation of manufacturing was the major announcement from *Foxcom.* Foxcom deployed a million robots to completely automate the manufacturing process.[83] Once this was completed, it was so easy to replicate and automate the manufacturing process. In the future, *Foxcom* 's advancements will become a template for new manufacturing plants. New plants will be able to outcompete old human labor plants so effectively that the downward pressure to automate all manufacturing processes will become a self-fulfilling prophecy. In a certain sense, it is surprising that it is only beginning now, and I suspect that it has only been due to the fact that the cost of a human life over a working lifetime is less than a robot's, until recently.

The good news is that I believe that the combination of robotics and renewable energy could bring back manufacturing to the US with a vengeance. The costs of a robotic factory in the US and China are practically the same. Most consumption comes from the USA anyway.[84] However, there are also well-oiled manufacturing supply chains into China which will take some time to readjust back to the United States. But, once robotic manufacturing takes hold in the USA, how can China compete? As long as the regulatory and taxation policies of the US are progressive or even developed to encourage this type of manufacturing, then manufacturing in the USA will explode. However, the jobs won't, and it is likely that workers, states and elected officials will perceive this as a threat to their already meager manufacturing jobs. Politicians will most likely react initially by providing a challenging environment for robotic manufacturing. This kind of shortsighted protectionism will not disrupt what could be a massive boom for the US economy for a great deal of reasons which include short term job growth, innovation and competitiveness. This kind of protection legislation happens more often than you think. You only have to look at *Tesla* cars, which certain people mocked as a pie in the sky fantasy, only to turn around and try to ban them because they are out selling traditional dealerships.[85]

The robotic technology will not be there yet to build these plants without human labor, so the massive labor requirements for building this new sector will be huge. Secondly, if you can combine new robotic manufacturing with renewable energy, you effectively have zero operating cost manufacturing plants. Material costs will become the main component to manufacturing costs, as well as a small overhead to cover the financing of the equipment, and building the initial technology and then operating it over 20-30 years.

This will have one very beneficial effect on the US economy, as it did when industrialization first took place. The cost of goods will plummet. You may think that the percentage of labor costs for a given item is relatively small. For example, an iPhone's labor costs are around 2-5% of its manufacturing costs .[86] But as more and more parts of the industry become mechanized, every process to achieve the end product drops. Material costs will drop by 10 %, component costs will drop 10%, assembly costs will drop 10%, and quality assurance will drop 10%. Then, if you start adding in automated logistics and robotic mining, you really begin to have a massive impact on costs throughout the process. Each process you automate you're lowing costs, but you are also removing massive amounts of jobs. Every robotic cloud has a dark lining when it comes to jobs.

It should also increase the quality of the products we use every day significantly. The great aspect about robotics is that there is no room for mistakes. A robot knows if it is within 0.1% of standard quality, and it will adjust or put itself into repair accordingly. Of course, with ultra-high resolution cameras and pattern recognition technology at the end of the process, even a hair out of place will be spotted in milliseconds.

While these robots will be specialists in their tasks, there is a trend towards multifunction manufacturing bots. Like human operators who use specialist machines, it is likely that robots will be flexible enough so that one type of robotic manufacturing machine can perform a multitude of manufacturing jobs.

This robotic revolution is on the verge of beginning. *Rethink Robotics* recently launched "Baxter", a rather friendly looking robot that can perform a huge range of manufacturing tasks. Most importantly, "Baxter" can learn new tasks without any technical input. Basically, a co-worker can guide "Baxter" to perform an action, and it will simultaneously learn the necessary process. Furthermore, "Baxter" can work alongside humans in the production line with its advanced safety features, which means that its human colleagues will slowly see themselves replaced. *Rethink Robotics* does not try to hide the fact that the product is designed to make costs for small businesses around the same level as Chinese labor or, as they like to put it, "makes US manufacturing competitive again". The other incredible characteristic of "Baxter" is that it has a low price tag of around $22,000. When you factor in the economic benefits of robotic labor purchasing it becomes a no-brainer. Now, obviously Baxter is not quite as dexterous as the human hand, but those advances will come.

Another such robot from *ABB*, which, again, has been given a very friendly name, *Freda* (which surprise, surprise, is an acronym [for Friendly Robot for Industrial Dual-arm Assembly). *Freda* is designed to be able to work alongside humans and is officially touted to "ameliorate" or "alleviate" labor shortages. In reality, this is basically a bullshit way of trying to make people comfortable with the idea of a robot replacing low-skilled low-paid jobs. Economics are the only real factor in loses of low-skilled jobs. It is always possible to find labor at the right price, so all that robots will do is place a downward pressure on wages. From a business perspective, it is easy to evaluate. Let's do the sums. I have been involved in a long-term asset of finance, and it won't be long before someone puts together a financial package that looks a little like the one shown below. In fact, it might even be mine!

Human Industrial Labor (US)

Average Work Week Hours = 43 Hours

Average pay inc benefits = $31.79 [87]

Total lifetime cost of a human worker over 25 years excluding inflation = $ 1,777,061

Robot Labor

Number of hours a week = 334 (working 100% faster with 1 hour downtime)

Cost of robot = $200,000

Maintenance, parts, electricity @ 10% per year = $20,000

Total lifetime cost of a robot worker over 25 years excluding inflation = $700,000

**Robot's hourly rate = $1.61 or almost 2000% lower cost than a human equivalent.**

On the following page, the graph shows how cost effective robots are against human labor even if they work the same shifts. Thus, in order to make robot labor work, the capital cost of the robot replacing the human could still cost a staggering $5 million. At this price, it would still be more cost-effective than the human equivalent. The real problem for human labor is that these multifunction robots are more likely to cost around the $200,000 mark and will drop rapidly in price to the point where they can replace a human job with the capital cost of only one year's worth of salary. Even if you take the model to Chinese labor costs at $1.36 an hour, you can still make the financial model work if the capital cost of the robot is under $250K.[88]

This does not even take into account the costs savings for the additional cost of maintaining a human work force, such as canteens and reduced property footprint. Who knows, these robots may even work in the dark!

So we build this amazing manufacturing utopia. Of course, this will be an initial boom for jobs, not just in building factories, but also in research, development and ongoing maintenance. However, these will most likely only span a decade or so. You see, while at the moment these robots will initially need maintenance and repair from humans, we are about to open the door to the first technology since biology, in which the robots will repair themselves. We are not there yet, but we do not have to stretch our imaginations much to see that robots have the future capability to build, disassemble, diagnose and repair each other as well.

I mean, after all, there isn't a single industrial robotic manufacturer that would be able to get away with asking others to automate production lines without totally automating its own.

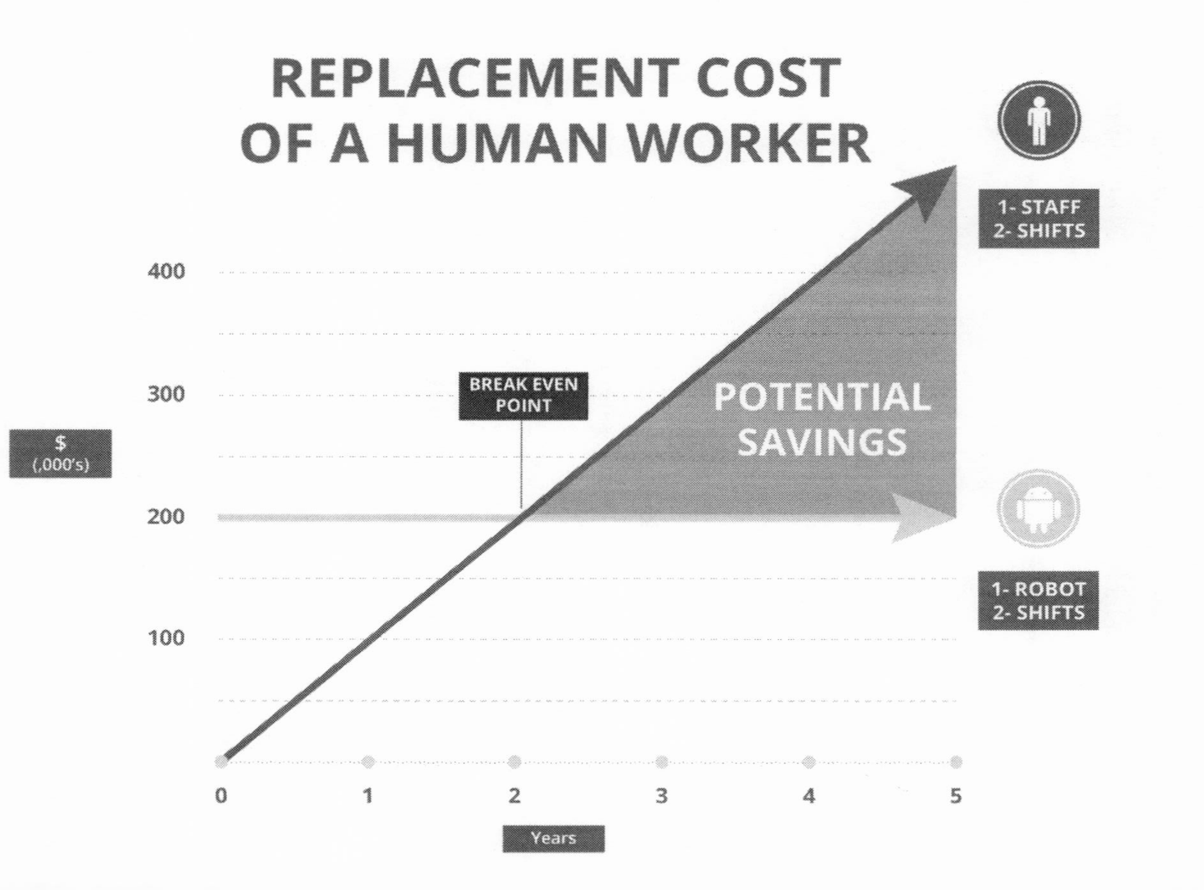

REPLACEMENT COST
OF A HUMAN WORKER
1- STAFF
2- SHIFTS
1- ROBOT
2- SHIFTS
POTENTIAL
SAVINGS
BREAK EVEN
POINT
$
(,000's)
400
300
200
100
0
1
2
3
4
5
Years

So, we get to the point where robots are building other robots, and it is obvious that there is something unnerving about that idea.

It is also important to recognize that manufacturing as a whole could eventually disappear completely. We are already developing quite advanced 3D printers. Some can build full color models, while others can build highly detailed shapes, electronics, and even build body parts for us faulty humans.[89, 90, 91]

As these technologies develop into full-on build-it bots, construction and assembly of high-quality complex products becomes possible. Initially, we will use it for novelty items, toys (watch out *Lego*!) and replacement parts. However, as technologies become able to integrate multiple materials together, they will begin to replace more low-level products, just as robots will take lower tiers of higher and higher level jobs out of the market. 3D printing will take out lower tiers of products away from manufacturing. Soon, it will be possible to replicate almost anything through 3D printing. This will increase the impact that robotics will have on manufacturing, and obviously printing at home means complete exclusion from logistics and retail. Even those who generate income from the creative process of developing 3D products will face challenges, as product piracy becomes a major issue. I really have no idea how the likes of *Lego* will be able to protect itself against intellectual property theft. There have been calls already for the DRM (digital rights management) to be at the core of 3D printing.[92] When people began to build parts of guns on 3D printers, they were deleted from sharing sites.[93] However, as we have seen time and time again, whenever products have DRM applied, people have found ways of sharing and circumventing them. With physical products, it could become even more complicated, as you have the ability to place data within the product itself. A finely applied pattern on the outside of the brick, containing the data required to replicate the brick, could be photographed and instantly converted into a copy of that product. 3D scanners already exist and allow you to scan a 3D object and print an identical copy from a 3D printer. It would be almost impossible to stop this replication.

Then of course you have to ask where this will stop. Will it ever reach a point like *Star Tre*k where your friendly 3D 'replicator' can conjure anything you want through simple commands?, Or, maybe 3D printers will be at the core of military combat, with thousands of drones being produced in the field in an infinite loop of destruction. Will robots themselves eventually be able to reproduce in the womb of a 3D printer?

# CHAPTER 10: BEING PROBED, DIGITAL DOCTORS AND NUMERIC NURSES

Everything I have discussed until this point is based off the principle that low-level jobs will be replaced by robotics first, as simple tasks are easier to replicate. The medical profession is the one exception to this rule for a very simple reason. The medical sector is ridiculously expensive and inefficient. If there is one sector that needs to be mechanized for our future survival, it's medicine. These changes are already starting to occur around the edges of the industry.

It's not even that we humans are that efficient in medical care. It is estimated that 1.5 million patients will come to harm per year from preventable medical mistakes.[94] We are human and we make mistakes. Robots can generate errors, but they do not make mistakes.

There are so many opportunities to revolutionize medical care through robotics in the short and long term future. Medicine is one of the hardest industries to predict the future of robotic technology.

Robotics has started to make its way into the medical sector. The *Da Vinci* was the first robotic medical device to be approved by the FDA in 2000.[95] The *Da Vinci* looks like a robot that is going to kill you by lethal injection rather than a robot that will perform surgery on you. But, while the promise of being able to use it remotely to allow the top surgeons in the world perform complicated surgeries over thousands of miles, it has not been embraced in the same way as the creators had originally intended.[96] Even though the robot has many advantages in being able to perform less intensive surgeries, the reality is that the technology is expensive and cumbersome, and human surgeon need to invest a considerable amount of time learning how to manipulate the *DaVinci* to the fullest effect. However, this has not stopped companies from aggressively developing in this space. This includes a great deal of technologies such as the heavy duty *Epoch*, which looks like some technology out of a space odyssey. This has been described as "a major step toward the goal of exceeding the human hand". Another type of surgical technologies include lightweight surgical assistants such as *Freehand*, which provides the surgeons with a spare pair of hands .

Almost every robotic company knows that there is a veritable goldmine in medical robotic care. *iRobot* quickly went from creating military products, then consumer products, and finally medical products, with the release of *Vita*, an upgrade of an earlier robot from another company they acquired. However, the Vita is not even that innovative. It's basically an *iPad* on wheels with a great deal of fancy sensors that allow physicians to remotely control and interact with their patients in the ward without ever seeing them face-to-face.

Despite these new developments, most of the robots being developed today leave humans in the loop. The real revolution will occur when we realize that leaving our life in the hands of a robot is the safest thing to do. This realization is already beginning. The digital star of Jeopardy, IBM's *Watson*, is currently on a mission to acquire all existing medical knowledge in order to provide better doctors with better suggestions for treatment and diagnostics of conditions.[97] Once *Watson* is educated and completed, it will be safer to enter your symptoms, vitals and test results into *Watson* than to consult a real doctor. Of course, just as in flying, humans will not be able to let go of that psychological need to have a human at the sharp end of decision-making. However, economics will again force our hands. You see, without robotics and technology replacing doctors and nurses, the cost of healthcare will continue to rise significantly and we will all suffer. Medicine has allowed us to survive much longer than our biology should allow us to. I plan to live until I am at least 150 years old, but in order to do so, I must find a way of maintaining my biological body at a cost that is less than the productivity I generate. Otherwise, I am in a deficit to society. With essentially every person in the western world taking advantage of the new life expectancy, it can only mean one thing: bankruptcy. Therefore, I do not only see robotics in medicine as a benefit to humanity. I believe that it is a critical requirement for our survival. As many jobs as we will lose through robotics, by automating the requirements of being human, food, drink and health, we may just find ourselves in a position in which the cost of maintaining a person in society becomes so low that it does not require the same productivity as the present. After all, we all know that based upon primary demographics, not enough young people are replacing the retired work force.[98] The aspects that are always ignored in this argument are the changing basic cost dynamics of society. If robotics truly does free us up to provide exceptional medical care and low-cost nutrition and shelter, then there is hope.

Nursing is another area in which patient care will become less and less relevant. As the automation of diagnostic care becomes easier and more efficient, patients will begin to have full-time diagnostic monitoring that will provide detailed real-time diagnostic and blood work information. This, combined with the new wave of much safer needleless injections, makes nurses becomes less and less relevant.[99] Nurses will find that they can cover a much wider range of patients with a much smaller number of responsibilities. Initially, nurses' jobs may actually become more demanding as telepresence puts pressure on nurses to check physical conditions of patients, but as the technologies above mature there is no doubt that the number of nurses required will decline significantly. However, most likely a long period time will pass before they are no longer needed altogether.

Beyond robotics, technologies are developing that will allow us to live exceedingly long lives with, most importantly, a better quality of life. No one wants to spend the last twenty years of their 150 year life in a hospital. Technology will provide this, but older people are still an issue, and not just because they occasionally become grumpy. Care for the elderly and infirm is a big business, but any one who has been to a mediocre or poor care home, or has looked after an elderly person, knows that the situation is pretty grim. Care homes are notoriously bad in their care techniques for a good reason. The economics simply do not work. Providing the best care at the lowest possible cost are two conflicting and incompatible goals. Care bots to the rescue! Yes, this will most likely be the first area where real everyday human/robot interaction will come. There are many reasons for this. Firstly, the elderly are lonely, and studies have shown that robotic interaction is a form of interaction that stimulates, which increases happiness and probably reduces dementia.[100,101] The bottom line is that a great number of people in care are lonely and devoid of human interaction. A robot could be the next best solution to an absence of human attention. The other great

characteristic of a robotic helper is that they are the most amazing alarm clock. People forget medicines. In fact, we have developed a compliance device called the *Clever Cap* that alarms, dispenses and tracks compliance to taking medicines.[102] The compliance record is sent back to doctors who prescribe the medication. It is estimated that this problem alone costs the US 289 billion dollars a year.[103] A robotic helper will be the *Clever Cap* on steroids, reminding and dispensing medicine without fail. This is also an area where robotic super strength will come into its own. Infirm, ill or disabled humans are really, really difficult to move around. It can take up to three people to pick up the deadweight of a human. A genius at *Riken Robotics* worked out that building a robot to do this relatively simple task would be quite useful, so they came up with the *RIBA*, a rather friendly looking robot that can lift and move a human around with ease.[104] What we are likely to find is the development of super friendly care robots that perform a wide range of care options for the elderly and infirm. I suspect that for a great deal of people, these robots will be a literal lifesaver, and improve emotional and physical quality of life in one relatively low-cost robot. The benefits for society will be huge. Home care will last for much longer and be much lower in cost. Those who do move into care homes can be monitored 24 hours a day, not only by their care workers, but also by friends and family.
Communication will become easier as the robots will be able to learn behavior patters and even communicate the emotional and psychological state to close ones. "Grandma needs a virtual hug," could become a regular message. Already we are starting to see the initial products coming to market in this space. I am assisting a company called *Roambotics,* which has built a small low cost

robot, lovingly named *Junior* . *Junior* allows non intrusive automated home monitoring. In the future you won't have to say, "I've fallen and I can't get up" . Junior will have already called the paramedics.

Robots will be able to monitor their patients in so much detail unobtrusively, from monitoring their heart rate to detecting behavior change, dietary requirements, and sleep patterns[105]. These robotic care takers will most likely be able to pick up health issues even before they arise, immediately be able to evaluate the next steps, and provide a great amount of preventative care, thus lowering costs and distress over the span of interaction. The cost of these devices will probably become part of a healthcare structure or pension plan, as it makes sense to finance these devices in the same way pensions are spread over an expected lifespan. Thus, the cost to the end user is minimal. Additionally, don't forget that the useful lifespan of these robots could be upwards of thirty years.

Psychology is another area in which robotic development is rapidly gaining ground. As *Apple* realized, in order to create an amazing product, it needed to develop form and function of that product. Robot manufactures now recognize that (especially in the field of medicine and psychology) the outward appearance of a robot is essential to user adoption. Not only does a robot need to look friendly, but it also needs to act in a friendly manner and engage with human psychology so that humans trust it. "Trust" is a funny word when it comes to robots, given that they are just a collection of inputs, rules and outputs. However, "trust" underpins a great deal of our interactions with both people and objects. We feel uncomfortable when we walk onto a thirty year old propeller plane that creaks, despite our lack of knowledge regarding whether it is safe or not. Therefore, perception, especially in care, is critical. This is why a large number of care bots that are already starting to hit the market place look (well, there is no other way to say this) 'cute.' Maybe it's because a lot of them come from Japan and have been inspired by too many *Hello Kitty* adverts.

Care providers make up a highly skilled part of the workforce, which is one area in which not all care worker jobs will be lost. I suspect that human care workers will primarily concern themselves with adding that last bit of quality of life to an individual. Rather than spending a huge amount of time with one person, or sorting out the mundane, which the robot will have already completed, care workers will be free to build upon the human--robot relationship and simply provide that extra interaction. This, of course, is as long as society can still afford it.

Mental health is another area where robots can really help on a therapeutic level. Mental health is a very subjective specialist field, and I suspect that this field of work will endure over a long period of time, especially on the research side. It will be a little while until we completely unravel the mystery of the brain. Though with the $1 billion check that the European Union just wrote to create a digital replica of the human brain, who knows![106] Psychological treatment in all but the worst cases tends to be a very fragmented and a drawn out process. If you're lucky, you might see your shrink once a week and they may give you some homework. But, given how disabling, distressful and destructive to quality of life, anything to speed up the process and create more engagement in treating the problem becomes a very constructive exercise. The first real demonstration of a robot specifically designed for psychological benefit is the very cuddly *Paro* robot, modeled after a baby seal. *Paro* responds very much in the same way as any pet would.[107] Being able to respond to touch and stimuli in a soft cuddly way, *Paro*'s psychological benefits are similar to that of owning a pet. As these become more advanced, such bots will be able to take people on therapy journeys in ways that a psychologist cannot. These therapeutic sessions will be interactive. As the robot learns the therapeutic effects, it will modify and enhance its interaction to give the best results. The robot can then flag or relay significant changes in behavior back to the psychologist. These will especially be useful for short-term issues such as post-traumatic stress, where even early symptoms and signs can make significant differences to the end outcome.[108] I am not sure that we will see soldiers walking around a battlefield with a *care bear* in their backpack, but maybe they should.

The other major benefit these robots have, when it comes to mental health, is that they will be able to remove the stigma of seeing a psychologist if they are ashamed of their condition. These robots will be seen as completely neutral and non-judgmental.

While we talk about robotic doctors and nurses and surgeons, we still imagine a hospital or a doctor's office. While specialist care centers will exist primarily for access to specialized equipment or drugs, most medical interaction will be far more personalized. Telemedicine is already having an impact, and humans now have far more control over their health than ever before.[109] As we have been provided with increasing access to information, we have started to become our own practitioners, diagnosing and analyzing our own symptoms before deciding to go to the doctor.[110] As self diagnostic tools become more prevalent, and as sensors become common additions to the devices we take around with us all the time, we will increasingly rely on our own diagnostics first before seeing a doctor.[111] It will become highly unlikely that you will actually visit a doctor first before other forms of diagnosis. The first step in this process has already begun. Medical booth technology is currently in the process of development. With a host of low-cost hyper-efficient fluid diagnostic technologies coming to market, a quick pop to your local supermarket's medical booth will be all you will need to diagnose 95% of all medical problems.[112,113] As these booths become more sophisticated, there is no reason why they could not dispense prescription drugs (maybe they will include a sex bot in the booth as a diagnostic test before they dispense any *Viagra!*), and even provide some basic procedures such as mole removal. What about a 3D printed cast when you break your arm?

What would the reaction be from the medical community when this method replaces the present forms of diagnostics and monitoring? If you haven't already seen it, there's this new service/product (as of the writing of this book) that's from *Dr. Scholl's.* Basically, you step up to the machine and it measures exactly which product you need to relieve the pain in your feet. It's quite simple compared to what might be possible with such technology, but in the future, anything is possible. Imagine getting a scan of yourself at the pharmacy that will check to see which preventive actions you need to take for your health. It could determine whether or not you're in risk of a disease, fever, cold or anything. Furthermore, it'll allow you the ability to order that product and/or give you specialist doctors' contact information for your particular ailment.

I suspect that this type of advanced booth technology with robotic treatment will gain ground in poorer economies first before transitioning into developed economies. This is a shame, given the potential benefit that these booths would bring to a lower income part of society, where medical care is often forsaken until it becomes a major health issue.[114]

If the U.S. government truly wants to lower medical care costs, it should incentivize and encourage technological innovation in the area of telemedicine and robotics. However, the realities are that too much red tape and lobbying will keep the costs of healthcare high for some years yet.

Perhaps, medical bots will develop another level of sophistication by which they'll be available for emergency response work. The diversity and challenges of real world emergencies will be one of the most challenging areas for robotics to develop and could take a long time to achieve. While the benefits of having automated emergency medical response would be beneficial both in decreased response time and the diversity of treatment options, it is fair to say that a human will need to be in the loop in the near future. In fact, the first robotic emergency response technologies will most likely be firefighting UAV's.[115]

I have discussed how robotics will impact the medical profession, but really the medical professions is all about disease-care, not healthcare. If we really want to improve our long-term health outcomes, we must spend much more time on preventative measures. We are already seeing how technology can drive behavior change. As we gain more control and visibility over our day-to-day lives with the likes of the *Nike Fuel Band*, the *Ignite* pad (that my sister and I developed last year which allows you to objectively measure your fitness and weight), and more detailed and invasive tests including *WellnessFX* and *23andMe*, we are learning more about our physiology every day.

As predictive medicine becomes more accurate and more detailed, we should be able to the reach the stage where complete automated blood analysis is no more invasive than a glucose test. Armed with this knowledge, we will be able to make health decisions almost immediately in an attempt to try and mitigate any future health problems. This, combined with far more information on our dietary inputs (you are what you eat), may actually significantly reduce the burden on the healthcare system. An interesting health insurance plan would be that which effectively taxes everything you place into your body. Based upon your physiology and with technology like *Google Glass* tracking your every move, would you trade your dietary and exercise privacy for a massive reduction in premiums? When these economic incentives start to appear, people who cannot accept that privacy is dead will most likely find their premiums increasing significantly. But, for those who find it hard to adjust to behavior change, there still is hope. This will come in the form of behavior bots, specifically designed to track and motivate and drive behavior change. These bots will do an even better job than my personal trainer in motivation. It will know exactly what motivates you, whether that is a nice cold beer at the end of a workout or a cash incentive provided by your insurance company. Behavior bots will not just train you. They will monitor you until you hit your goals. They will work together with your other technological devices and social networks to provide non-stop enticement to make you healthier. These could be some very annoying robots. Those who cannot accept either will end up having to pay out of pocket for medical treatment, so let's hope those bot doctors are cheap.

# CHAPTER 11: ENTERTAINMENT AND THE FUNNY BOTS

Everything until this point has predicted robots replacing humans because of bots higher functionality and lower cost than their human equivalents. But, could robots start to take over some of the creative aspects of entertainment and the arts? Is that even possible, considering the individuality and "humanness" that creativity entails and is inherent of? Perhaps, for robots, it's the world of creative arts that's really the last frontier. After all, any type of art is subjective to the enjoyer, and perhaps then the possibility of the provider of that enjoyment need not be human. Of course, there is also the question of originality in some sense; if a robot performs or creates something for artistic enjoyment, isn't it simply programmed knowledge and not creativity that allows that robot to innovate? Is there a sense of creative thinking, originality, and a certain sense of individualistic input to be wanting if it is the creator of the robot who is the person that develops the robot's creativity? Copyright and intellectual property may even need to be modified, if a robot comes up with an original idea, then who owns it? Well, if anything, there is no doubt that robots generate general interest in entertainment from films like *AI* and *I, Robot* to television programs like *Robot Wars.*

There is an innate fascination between the superiority of humans and robots. This has been demonstrated by the amazing trivia knowledge of IBM's *Watson* and the superior chess skills of *Deep Blue.*[116] It is unlikely to stop there. Imagine the possibilities of mental tournaments between humans and robots for your viewing pleasure on television. *Watson* on the ever popular show *Jeopardy* has proven interest in humans being challenged and challenging robots and artificial intelligence. Maybe such a craze might catch on. Considering the many reality shows widely available and considering their inexplicable popularity, perhaps such shows that exploiting robots might be a breath of fresh air for viewers seeking a more intellectually stimulating experience.

I'm not suggesting that robots are going replace writers' or artists' jobs, even though there has been some development in automated music creation. More so, technology could start to replace not the original creative ideas, but the expression of them. We have already started to see this happen in the movie world, where actors are becoming digitized and lending only their voices and image to the movie, rather than their acting skills.[117] Currently, the technology is not quite there to completely replicate real world actors in digital scenes, but the technology is not far from it either. We have already found a way to seemingly bring back the dead and interact with us in a convincing way when a holographic Tupac preformed on stage.[118] As this and other technologies develop the blur between film, video game and real life, the realistic entertaining experience will become ever greater. The current stars of today may be immortalized digitally, it will be possible for them to star in films long after they die. New actors will find it increasingly hard to become a known entity in their own right, as more and more production is moved to pure digital production.

Robots will also be able to perform a host of creative arts perfectly. As we have seen with the popularity of wax museums, there is enjoyment even in static interaction with inanimate objects that represent the individuals we idolize. Robotics will be able to take this to the next stage. Want Madonna to sing at your next birthday? Just hire the Madonna bot. She will tirelessly perform every number perfectly accompanied with her robotic band.

This could be a real challenge for aspiring musical artists that rely on informal gigs and covers to make some money while they are following their art. Once fully humanoid robots start to hit the market, they will be able to play a whole multitude of instruments. Simply ask them, and they will download the professional violin skill from their app store. Live music at dinner may become fashionable again.

There is no doubt that we will also build robots that can create amazing art. We have already started to explore this concept with robots that can paint, including bots that can paint your dreams.[119,120] What will happen when a robot can look at your existing art, predict what you will like, and download a very high resolution image combined with a 3D scan data of the face of a painting to calculate the exact brush strokes required to recreate it? Could this put an end to galleries and artistic prints?

*Disney* has not let the entertainment aspects of robotics pass them by. In fact, *Disney* has its own robotics research department. Its *Imagineering* research and development arm conjurers up all kinds of strange and wonderful animatronics, including a rather stiff-looking Obama giving a speech in the Disney Hall of Presidents.[121] Given that Disney first started using animatronics in 1961, it is actually surprising that they are not further ahead on the interactivity side of robotics. This is beginning to change as they have developed a rather scary looking juggling/catch bot for interactive engagement in their parks.[122] I suspect that this is only the beginning. Someone must be working on turning Pinocchio into a real boy.

What if robots start to transition into theatre as well? I still think that there will be an innate interest in human theatre, but opening up works of performing art to robotic actors that could be transported anywhere could be of significant educational benefit and create a new entertainment-led industry. Just imagine watching *Hamlet* recreated in perfect glory at your local school or park or even in your garden.

We will also see increasing robotic sports. This may be a combination of both human against robots, humans controlling robots, and robots against robots.

As was graphically depicted in the film *AI,* and given our interest in shows like *Robot Wars*, robot on robot combat is likely to provide great entertainment value. This is especially true considering that the range of robots will increase and 3D printing will rapidly reduce the cost of repair. Given the right format, this could actually be an interesting driver for technical development, just as *Formula 1* has helped developed a great deal of the technical innovations we see in cars. A serious league-based robotic competition with significant revenues behind it would drive great innovation and would most likely be keenly observed by the U.S. military.

Time will show how this will affect jobs in the entertainment industry and the industries that depend on it. Robotics could replace many replicable forms of art and entertainment. I also suspect that as robots free up many hours in of our daily lives, the entertainment sector will grow significantly as we need to fill this time with endless entertainment. Much depends on to what extent full digital emersion technologies develop and how much time people will want to spend in the real world compared to a virtual one.

# CHAPTER 12: SLAVERY 2.0 AND WHEN BOTS GO WRONG

Let's say that if we get it right and robots free us as we enslave them, should we feel immoral that we have an army of autonomous slaves required to do their duty for us? After all, the dictionary defines slavery as *"The state of one bound in servitude as the property of a slaveholder or household."* One could argue that this only applies to humans. However, when people of color were brought into slavery, they were not considered "human" in the eyes of the government or slave owners. Instead, they were considered as not much more than animals. I don't personally think that robots are slaves because ultimately they do not 'feel' or obtain consciousness (at least for a while!), but I suspect that won't stop the debate from taking place. We humans become very attached to inanimate objects, so imagine how attached we will become to objects that interact with us and seemingly have a personality. Will we simply be able to throw out our childhood robot or will the grieving process be similar to the loss of a pet? It is quite possible that people will become so attached or fall in love with their sex bot, that they will care more about it than the humans around them.

I believe that relatively soon we will be able to program robots to believe they are alive. You only have to look at the *Turing Test*, in which the whole goal is to create a technology that is so indistinguishable from a human that we cannot tell it apart from the real being.[123] If we are this obsessed already, it won't be very long before this is applied to robotics. It starts to get complicated when a robot starts to beg you not to turn it off.

How will we react in the future when we must deal with this as a species? How will the manufacturers incorporate humanity into the personality of robots? After all, you have two competing challenges: you want a robot to seem as human as possible so that people feel like they understand and trust it, but at the same time you want it to be completely subservient.

The real challenge is when you actually build a learning robot that believes it is alive to the point it perceives that it should not be turned off. Some people would say this is consciousness, but in reality, it is not. It is a collection of rules that have made it come to a decision. While this is a dangerous state for a technology to be in, it must not be considered conscious. To be considered conscious, it must be a blank slate; it must learn from information and interaction around it just as a human does.

Actually, maybe I should come up with my own version of the *Turing Test* and deem it the "Way Test" which defines robotic consciousness as "The ability to express a fear of not existing without any predefined rules or knowledge." If this test is ever achieved, which I suspect at some point in the distant future it will be, then it will be the end of human intellectual dominance as we know it. We may well become no more than a cute cuddly species that the robot intelligence looks after like a pet.

We actually need to create some fundamental rules, as the recognition of our humanity should make it impossible to give robots any rights. As soon as we do give robots legal rights and view them as sentimental beings, we create a very slippery and dangerous route for humanity to potentially diminish. It will be an impossible process to stop once it starts. Why would we give robots rights? Well, it will be a very human behavior to begin with. Imagine a scenario in which one person assigns emotions to a robot and that is then abused. Maybe it's a rape of somebody's sex bot or a kick to a robot dog. Once people assign human qualities to a robot, they will naturally want to protect that robot beyond what current property laws allow.

Will it ever get to a point where robots will stand up for their rights or even go on strike to their human masters? I suspect that given the way most robots will be developed and controlled through corporations, it is very unlikely that they would ever let their creations get to a point where this could become an issue. The robots that will give us the most trouble will be experimental or open source robots that have less predefined rules and the ability to assimilate information at will. There are a great deal of possibilities here. Of course, it might come down to the whole concept and scope of artificial intelligence and "evolutionary" chips that I have mentioned in earlier chapters.

Even if robots had the potential to recognize their own consciousness, how can one be sure if a robot considers itself under the servitude of humans? Does a dog consider itself a pet or simply does it simply fulfill its duty to survive? Will a robot, if it ever does develop feelings, consider its identity in the same way, or will it began to develop more complex emotions? Such complex emotions could lead to an ersatz evolution in which the robot considers itself superior to humans, both in intellectual intelligence and emotional intelligence. If this is the case, will it then have malignant thoughts and feelings towards humans?

Well, if a robot ever did become human-like, I'm sure it might be brought to do evil deeds of its own accord, whether such deeds are out of malignant emotions or self-defense. This could open up a great deal of legal and ethical questions; I dare say it would redefine the whole concept of ethics and morals by incorporating this new phenomenon.

This has similar connotations to the debate that we have about the possibility of other advanced life forms existing. Would these life forms crush us like ants, leave us to our own devices or help us grow as a species? Maybe I have digested too much *Star Trek,* but fundamentally I believe that any advanced life form would have developed empathy. Therefore, I see no reason that a robot that has achieved conscious would not have the same or more empathy as a human. You might disagree that humans have great empathy, giving our violent past. However, if you provide humans with the means to live comfortably, we tend to look after each other and other 'less' intelligent life forms quite well.

Corporate robots will be heavily monitored and controlled. That's not to say that they won't go wrong. It will be very interesting to see who gets lumbered with the liability once robotics really takes off. If robots have the ability to learn and go beyond their original programming, and a robot accidentally kills someone is it the original programmer, the corporation, the person that taught them or the end user that is liable? At least the lawyers won't be losing their jobs!

Another serious problem will be hacking and viruses. As we enter an era of cyber terrorism, it is quite possible that robots will become a primary target for mischief. The potential multitude of issues that comes with having a physical device that has multiple sensors and facets should not be underestimated. As robots become part of our everyday lives, the ability for illegal surveillance becomes irresistible. The possibility of interference or utilizing robots to carry out terrorist actions becomes a real risk. It was only a few years ago that an 'unknown' state launched a virus on the nuclear control equipment in Iran. Imagine what they could have done if the entire place was robotic.

At some point, these risks will be realized. Hopefully the first few will not be catastrophic and we can learn some valuable lessons regarding how to protect ourselves from such risks. However, if cyber warfare is anything to go by, it will be an uphill struggle.

# CHAPTER 13: ROBOT HUMANS AND BIONICS

It may not match your beliefs, but as our understanding of neurology and biology develop, it becomes quite clear that we are not much more than a very sophisticated machine. Humanity is in the process of modifying itself to become more like machines. At the same time, we are creating machines to embody human characteristics.

We are now reaching a point in biology in which we can combine invasive computer technology and biology together in ways that can not only just repair, but also enhance our natural capabilities. We already have the *Bionic Eye*, which I suspect will exceed the capabilities of a human eye in the next few decades. [124] Mice have been developed that are able to telepathically communicate with one another. From this, we begin to delve into a realm where biological modification becomes as common as plastic surgery. We can even augment our senses in ways that start to seem like magic.[125]

Great innovation is coming from solutions for those who need it the most. We are now seeing all kinds of body parts replaced by robotic counterparts. Bionic hands that can pick up potato chips, to leg frames that allow people to stand for the first time in years, are all part of this trend.[126,127] Combined with nano technology, it may be possible for robots to repair a being from the inside out and allow constant monitoring of failing organs.

It will not be that long before someone invents the "Google Chip" that can be connected directly into our cerebral cortex. It will allow us to access the entire world's information with a thought. If this sounds farfetched, then you only have to look at Professor Kevin Warwick who became the world's first 'cyborg' by implanting a chip that could control a robotic arm using the signals from his nervous system.[128]

Once humanity embarks down this route, it will be impossible to recover our humanity in the same way again. You might imagine that having the "Google Chip" implanted would be an optional procedure. Of course no one will force you to have it, but in reality, the economic and social pressures to have it will be immense. Just as those who initially resisted the internet or cell phones and eventually had to relent to their use, the same will be true for bio modifications. These bio modifications will be especially important to stay ahead of the robots, and it will be the only way in which we will be able to compete with our robotic counterparts for jobs.

Once this technology starts appearing, it becomes a self-fulfilling prophecy, just as it is no longer considered fair to restrict technology from children. When I have children and my son asks me, "Daddy, can I have the Google Chip?" my automatic response will be "No, you're too young." However, when I find out that his best friend has one and that my son is falling behind in school, then the pressure to get him one will become so great that I will probably end up allowing it. For those parents who are reading this, you have probably experienced a similar dilemma when it comes to mobile phones.

What will eventually start happening is that those who have bio-engineered themselves will have such an advantage in the employment sector that it will be almost impossible for those who have not bio-engineered themselves to find work. This will drive the pressure to bio-engineer even further to the point where there will be a split in the human species. Those who bio-engineer themselves will have greater opportunities and economic success. Those who do not will start to become a sub-species weighed down by their inferior human brain that cannot compete with its digital bio-engineered cousin.

This definitely embodies the characteristics of science fiction at the moment, but we must ask ourselves how we will deal with this as a species. We currently live in a fundamentally unfair society where the wealthy live longer, have more opportunities and receive a better education. This creates a self-fulfilling loop of more prosperity and economic freedom for the rich and deeper poverty for the poor. At the moment, society seems to be able to deal with this inequality despite the London riots and the 99% movement. But, when your success and prosperity eventually become linked directly to the ability to bio-engineer yourself, then the divide becomes so much more obvious. As much as I am a believer in the capitalist society we live in, I am not sure how stable it will be once this becomes apparent.

Just like the internet and telephone, this type of technology will become a fundamental right (finally, a silicon implant for everybody!). Perhaps the cost of living will become so low that most people will be able to survive at an acceptable level without the technology. The advancement could evolve to the point where the cost of the chip and the robotic surgery to implant it both become extremely low.

Our current generation could be the last to remember what it was to be truly human. What difference would there be if our minds change as we are fully connected into the digital world? It has already been shown that the internet is changing the way we think and store information.[129] I mean, after all, a few hundred years ago, the most information we would consume in a day would be that Uncle George cut his toe from using the plough. That would have been the news for the next month! Human brains were never designed for the deluge of information we now consume on a daily basis. It is no wonder why more than ever larger parts of the population are having mental health issues.

The question of at which point technology becomes invasive is one that we are in the process of trying to answer, with the advent of *Google Glass,* we are having to evaluate not only the impact on us, but also the impact on the people around us.[130] *Google Glass* has caused an uproar because we have never had such an intrusive technology in public before. The outcome of how we accept or reject technology like this will likely have far reaching consequences for robotics. New technology has so many unintended consequences that it may be difficult for our society to catch up. Let's say that you are in a men's bathroom and forget to turn off your *Google Glass* and a child uses the urinal next to you. Even though you are not looking, your *Google Glass* is. Does this mean that you have suddenly become a child pornographer? Robots will face the same challenges; if a robot sees you wife break the law, will it have an obligation to report it? As our technologies converge with us, the line between our private and public life becomes more blurred. Perhaps robots will even know what we are thinking before we ourselves do.

This hybrid between machine and human technology could give us humans the edge on robots in creative and decision-making jobs. After all, if the robots are there to serve us, they cannot compete with a human brain with the biological processing power of a super computer and the raw power of silicon. Maybe we will always stay ahead of the curve, but this will most likely cause us to lose some aspects of our humanity in the process.

# CHAPTER 14: HUMANS AND THE CRUMBS LEFT FOR US

It may seem hopeless for us little humans, and you may be wondering what the future holds for us; bags of blood and bones that have created our entire life around our jobs.

The current generation is starting to feel the effects of this robotic future, but the real questions become: What will the future hold for our children? What should they learn? What career should they pursue? and, What does their future hold?

We must first make sure that technology in education keeps up with the dynamic changes that are happening around us. Children and education have to embrace these changes with open arms; children need to be at the cutting edge of technology, as it will most likely define their future.

We also have to use these technologies to lower the cost of living for all parts of society. If we fail to achieve this and our society does become more polarized, then social unrest is bound to happen as people become discontent with the status quo and rightly so. Society, at least, has to believe that there is equal opportunity for everyone. That is the American Dream, but as we have seen with the 99% protests, this can be easily eroded in times of economic turmoil.

But for all our failings, we as a species do have some wonderful features as well. We strive for new knowledge and learning and we are exceedingly creative, two areas which I suspect will be impossible for technology to replicate. While we have a history of violence and mismanaged power, individually, I believe, most humans are kind and want to help our fellow man.

If we can embrace this and realize that the cost of looking after the many using robotics is better than just pampering the few, we should live in a much happier and stable society.

Governments should be doing everything they can to encourage the development of robotics and provide incentives or open up markets for robotic disruption as early as possible. As we have always seen with technology, once you have opened *Pandora's Box,* it is impossible to close it. The technology is coming. We can't stop that. However, by embracing it, governments can direct the technology where it helps the many and not the few. Special incentives should be provided in which companies can show that they have reversed the outsourcing process, and have started to bring robotic labor and manufacturing into the country. This will drive additional high skilled jobs and increase productivity.

Industries that do not embrace it will be outcompeted by those who do. I know that there will be big companies that consider robotics a fad, and they will repeat the mistakes they made when they thought that the internet was a temporary fad for geeks and porn addicts.

Small and medium business owners should be looking at all aspects of low-skill level human labor and the cost of replacing it with robotic technology. Once the realization that this technology is not decades away, but can be accessed today, business owners need to stop considering this technology as far out and inaccessible. Soon, not having robotic technologies for business will be as strange as not having a website or an email address.

Finance will also play a critical role in robotics. I am already working on a finance leasing company for robotics that provides simple finance and rental programs for companies. This allows companies to access this technology without the high capital costs associated with the relatively expensive upfront investment in robotics.

As I have said before, the future I present here depends a great deal on how we approach the future together as a society. Maybe we will become like the Luddites and rebel against the technology. Or, maybe we will embrace it with open arms and realize that while these changes could be turbulent, the future with robotics is better than without them.

But overall, I suspect that we will screw up a lot of technologies before we get them right. I think that technology and access to the communication and information we have now has had the overall effect of liberalizing society. I believe it will continue to do so. Hard work is rewarded, but equally society pulls together to provide a basic safety net. If that safety net had not existed when I was diagnosed with dyslexia and provided a laptop, I most likely would not even be able to construct a sentence, let alone write a book. There is no doubt in my mind that more and more people will require a safety net because technology and robotics will have stripped them of their purpose. If we do not provide the education and opportunities for us to grow in this new environment, the cracks in society are likely to cascade into social unrest on a scale that has not been seen before in the developed world.

It is also likely that large parts of society will disappear into a digital realm that provides them more enjoyment and interaction than the real world. These people will do as little as they can to just survive in the real world, eat, drink and stay connected, simply so they can be who they want in the digital world.

As these changes occur, we will adjust over time to this new reality, just as we have adjusted to the massive changes technology has brought about in just a couple of generations. After all, we are very good at evolving and adaption.

As these transitions mature, I suspect that we will educate and concentrate on three aspects of humanity that robots will have a very hard job replicating.

The first is obvious, and that is creative pursuits. I am talking about pure creation. People who can create beauty from nothing will be highly sought after, whether that's in the field of art, music or writing. Those who are bold and can be unpredictable will make a refreshing change from the sanitized predictability of robotics. Also, those talents in which you have to apply or understand abstract concepts about humanity will prosper. Such positions in marketing, branding and advertising will be irreplaceable, as will highly skilled artists in industries like comedy, theatre and dance where we can appreciate the beauty in the challenge, not just the visual or aural experience.

The second area where humanity will have the edge is that of bringing disparate pieces of random information together to make decisions. While as technology will be able to evaluate huge amounts of information and make recommendations, the nuances' of humanity will mean that a human will at least be in the loop for a long time. This means most highly skilled managerial or decision-making positions will be around far into the future. This is one area where I think education should evolve to allow a much wider view of how the world fits together. Education is very compartmentalized and not much effort is employed to help students connect these disparate dots. In the real world, almost everything is connected to another in some way, and we need the next generation to be educated in such a way that they have a polymorphic view of the world.

The third area where humanity will still be relevant is that of ultra-specialization in cutting edge industries. While most fundamental information on almost anything will be available at the touch of a button, when it comes to new ideas and abstract thinking, the human brain is very powerful. Due to the trillions of unique connections in our brains, there will always be a need for human brains and thought.

In a nutshell, if I was a career advisor, I would be advising the children of the future to be as unique and free thinking as they can be. They need to understand the world in which they will live as much as they possibly can, be creative and drive that creativity into something that they are passionate about.

The one job that won't be replaced anytime soon is that of politicians. Representing humanity will be more important than ever, but let's face it: no robot could replace the inefficiency and madness of our government.

As we take this journey, there are two major risks for humanity that are interconnected. The first is that the rich and poor divide widens significantly, and the second is that those who have the money will use that money to improve their own biology, both through bioengineering and life extension. We will reach a point where not all humans are born equal even on a biological level, DNA will be manipulated and implants will be placed. Even if you have the natural ability to better yourself, it will be impossible to cross the rich-poor divide if you don't have the financial access to the bioengineering. Rich humans suddenly become super biologically enhanced humans, a higher race.

What happens to our society when that begins to occur and robots have taken all the normal human jobs? Will it only leave jobs for the super humans? That does not seem like a fair and just society.

We may even see certain parts of society break off and form their own informal robotic-less society very much like Amish have. Humans will be fatigued with technology, they will want breaks from it. Retreats and farming holidays could become a big recreational business. Just don't ask me to take my implant out and leave it at the door.

This is not a conversation to hide from. A great deal of robotic companies that I approached were very cautious or even resistant when talking about how their technology would impact jobs. This is understandable in a way, but this resistance is as pointless as it is to say that outsourcing jobs does not cause job losses. Many companies refuse to acknowledge the impact their creations have on the human race. Robots take jobs. That's a fact. It's not something to hide from, and the quicker we acknowledge and face that fact, the quicker we can move forward. One thing is for certain: whether they want acknowledge it or not, robotics is all about replacing human jobs.

Within the next thirty years, we will lose seventy percent of traditional jobs and they will not all be replaced by higher skill jobs. There is no doubt that this will cause social unrest and turbulence in society. But ultimately, when we come through the other side and as long as we maintain a society that is fundamentally fair, robotics should increase our quality of life, allow us to live longer and provide comforts that only very wealthy are privileged to experience today. Work will no longer be the center of our lives, and this change will allow us to concentrate on developing our artistic and intellectual side. It will hopefully usher in a new renaissance period for humanity. **The future is bright. The future is robotics.**

# BIBLIOGRAPHY

1 Rosheim, Mark. *Leonardo's Lost Robots.* Minnesota: Springer, 2006.Roudart,

2 Laurence, and Marcel Mazoyer. *A history of world agriculture.* Earthscan, 2006.

3 Aristotle. *The Politics of Aristotle.* Translated by E. Barker. Oxford University Press, 1961.

4 Ashton, T S. *The Industrial Revolution.* Oxford University Press, 1998.

5 Sale, Kirkpatrick. *Rebels Against The Future.* Basic Books, 1996.

6 Moore, Gordon E. *Cramming more components onto integrated circuits.* Electronics Magazine, 1965.

7 Charles R. Weisbin, Christopher Hawley, Bob Silberg. *Human-Robot System Architectures.* Nasa.gov, 2013.

8 Squeezing the electrons in: batteries don't follow Moore's Law. Deloitte, 2011.

9 Faraday, Michael. *On Some New Electro-Magnetical Motion, and on the Theory of Magnetism.* Royal Institution of Great Britain, 1822.

10 *Statistics Quarterly Results.* Japan Robot Association, 2012.

11 Rifkin, Jeremy. *The End Of Work.* Tarcher, 1994.

12 *Brynjolfsson, Erik. Race Against the Machine. Digital Frontier Press, 2012.*

13 Bureau of Labor and Statistics. "Occupational Employment Statistics." 2012.

14 Passel, Jeffrey, D'Vera Cohn, and Ana Gonzalez-Barrera. *Net Migration from Mexico Falls to Zero.* PewResearch, 2012.

15 Letcher, Trevor. *Climate Change: Observed impacts on Planet Earth.* Elsevier Science, 2009.

16 Blagdon, Jeff. *British company uses 3D printing to make stone buildings out of sand.* 2012. http://www.theverge.com/2012/2/21/2811146/3d-printing-d-shape-monolite-enrico-dini.

17 Borgobello, Bridget. *Yotel New York features world's first hotel robotic luggage handler.* 2011. http://www.gizmag.com/yotel-worlds-first-hotel-robotic-porter/19576/.

18 Grange, Lori. *Robot Trash Truck Picks Up Praise.* 1990. http://articles.latimes.com/1990-05-24/news/gl-204_1_garbage-truck.

19 Garun, Natt. *Are you a better artist than the Senseless Drawing Robot 2.* 2013. http://www.digitaltrends.com/lifestyle/are-you-a-better-artist-than-the-senseless-drawing-robot-2/.

20 Levy, David. *Love and Sex with Robots: The Evolution of Human-Robot Relationships.* Harper Perennial, 2008.

21 Leung, Isaac. *The Cultural Production of Sex Machines and the Contemporary Technosexual Practices.* RE/SEARCH, 2009.

22 Sher, Lauren. *Couple Celebrates 80th Wedding Anniversary, Shares Secrets to Lasting Marriage.* 2012. http://abcnews.go.com/US/john-ann-betar-celebrate-80th-wedding-anniversary-share/story?id=17769043#.UaKR-mRAT8Y.

23 Mccormack, David. *Porn study had to be scrapped after researchers failed to find ANY 20-something males who hadn't watched it.* 2013. http://www.dailymail.co.uk/news/article-2261377/Porn-study-scrapped-researchers-failed-ANY-20-males-hadn-t-watched-it.html#ixzz2Hxtetl62.

24 Mims, Christopher. *'Lovotics': The New Science of Engineering Human, Robot Love.* 2011. http://www.technologyreview.com/view/424537/lovotics-the-new-science-of-engineering-human-robot-love/.

25 Dmitry. *Doll Making: Behind the Scenes of Making Silicone Dolls.* 2011. http://designyoutrust.com/2011/09/doll-making-behind-the-scenes-of-making-silicone-dolls/.

26 Arthurs, Deborah. *The Skype is the limit!* 2012. http://www.dailymail.co.uk/femail/article-2141776/The-Skype-limit-Sex-toy-connects-laptop-lets-couples-hit-big-O-distance---novel-use-Nintento-Wii-remote.html.

27 Urmson, Chris. *The self-driving car logs more miles on new wheels.* 2012. http://googleblog.blogspot.hu/2012/08/the-self-driving-car-logs-more-miles-on.html.

28 Chan, Sewell. *Subways Run by Computers Start on L Line*

*This Summer.* 2005.
http://www.nytimes.com/2005/01/14/nyregion/14subway.html?_r=0.

29 Flint, Sunshine. *The futurist: Heathrow's personal transit pods.* 2011. http://www.bbc.com/travel/blog/20110922-the-futurist-heathrows-personal-transit-pods.

30 *2011 Commercial Vehicle Registrations Reach 1.25 Million, Led by Record Used Commercial Transactions, According to Polk.* 2012. http://www.prnewswire.com/news-releases/2011-commercial-vehicle-registrations-reach-125-million-led-by-record-used-commercial-transactions-according-to-polk-142617436.html.

31 Smith, Aaron. *Tons of trucking jobs ... that nobody wants.* 2012.
http://money.cnn.com/2012/07/24/news/economy/trucking-jobs/index.htm.

32 Scott, Katie. *Croatian entrepreneur unveils 190mph electric supercar.* 2011. http://www.wired.co.uk/news/archive/2011-09/13/rimac-electric-car.

33 Dreier, Hannah. *CHALLENGES REMAIN FOR CALIF. HIGH-SPEED RAIL PLAN.* 2012.
http://bigstory.ap.org/article/challenges-remain-calif-high-speed-rail-plan.

34 —. *Welcome To The Age of Pilotless Planes.* 2013.
http://www.usnews.com/news/articles/2013/05/13/britain-tests-pilotless-passenger-plane.

35 Griffin, Greg. *Human error is biggest obstacle to 100*

*percent flight safety*. 2010.
http://www.denverpost.com/ci_14398562.

36 Ukinski, Tom. *Drones: Mankind's Always Had Them*. 2013.
http://guardianlv.com/2013/05/drones-mankinds-always-had-them/.

37 Russell, Steve. *DARPA Grand Challenge Winner: Stanley the Robot!* 2006.
http://www.popularmechanics.com/technology/engineering/robots/2169012.

38 Reich, Robert. *America's biggest jobs program: The US military*. 2010. http://www.csmonitor.com/Business/Robert-Reich/2010/0813/America-s-biggest-jobs-program-The-US-military.

39 *Swarming Robots Could Be the Servants of the Future*. 2013. http://www.sheffield.ac.uk/news/nr/sheffield-centre-robotics-gross-natural-robotics-lab-1.265434.

40 *Star Trek: Voyager : The Swarm*. 1996.
http://www.imdb.com/title/tt0708989/

41 Barwick, Hamish. *Robot swarms could be used in search and rescue: expert*. 2013.
http://www.computerworld.com.au/article/457180/robot_swarms_could_used_search_rescue_expert_/.

42 Winerman, Lea. *Researchers Mine Cell Phone Data for Insight Into Human Behavior*. 2009.
http://www.pbs.org/newshour/updates/science/jan-june09/celldata_05-15.html.

43 Koebler, Jason. *Law Enforcement Blindsided By Public 'Panic' Over Drone Privacy.* 2013. http://www.usnews.com/news/articles/2013/03/21/law-enforcement-blindsided-by-public-panic-over-drone-privacy?page=2.

44 Blake, Matt. *G4S security guard sacked after he was found sleeping in entrance of hotel where Olympians are staying.* 2012. http://www.dailymail.co.uk/news/article-2175865/G4S-security-guard-sacked-sleeping-entrance-hotel-Olympians-staying.html.

45 Shand, Adam. *Human factor in need of help to defeat the flaws of CCTV.* 2013. http://www.theaustralian.com.au/news/nation/human-factor-in-need-of-help-to-defeat-the-flaws-of-cctv/story-e6frg6nf-1226639685367.

46 Hodson, Hal. "Robot inquisition keeps witnesses on the right track." *New Scientist,* 2013.

47 The Week. *South Korea's mood-sensing robotic prison guards.* 2012. http://theweek.com/article/index/226879/south-koreas-mood-sensing-robotic-prison-guards#.

48 Kyckelhahn, Tracey. *Justice Expenditures and Employment, FY 1982-2007.* U.S. Department of Justice , Bureau of Justice Statistics, 2011.

49 Hodson, Hal. *AI gets involved with the law.* 2013. http://www.newscientist.com/article/mg21829175.900-ai-gets-involved-with-the-law.html.

50 Osborne, Charlie. *Cybercrime costs U.S. consumers $20.7 billion.* 2012. http://news.cnet.com/8301-1009_3-57506216-

83/cybercrime-costs-u.s-consumers-$20.7-billion/.

51 Beckhusen, Robert. *Feds Drop $100 Million to Spot Flying, Homebrew Cocaine Mules.* 2012. http://www.wired.com/dangerroom/2012/08/ultralight/.

52 Harwood, Matthew. *Engineer Allegedly Offered Drug Smugglers Remote Controlled Semi-Submersibles.* 2009. http://www.securitymanagement.com/news/engineer-allegedly-offered-drug-smugglers-remote-controlled-semi-submersibles-005743.

53 Koba, Mark. *$2 trillion underground economy aids recovery.* 2013. http://www.usatoday.com/story/money/business/2013/05/12/2-trillion-dollar-underground-economy-recovery-savior/2144279/.

54 Fox News. *U.S. Army Tests Flying Robot Sniper.* 2009. http://www.foxnews.com/story/0,2933,517481,00.html.

55 Asimov, Isaac. *I, Robot.* Doubleday & Company, 1950.

56 Lilico, Andrew. *How the Fed triggered the Arab Spring uprisings in two easy graphs.* 2011. http://www.telegraph.co.uk/finance/economics/8492078/How-the-Fed-triggered-the-Arab-Spring-uprisings-in-two-easy-graphs.html.

57 Randerson, James. *Early chefs left indelible mark on human evolution.* 2003. http://www.newscientist.com/article/mg17723871.500-early-chefs-left-indelible-mark-on-human-evolution.html.

58 Lavelle, Marianne. *The Oil Drum: $100 a Barrel Quickens*

*the Beat.* 2008. http://money.usnews.com/money/blogs/beyond-the-barrel/2008/01/07/the-oil-drum-100-a-barrel-quickens-the-beat.

59 Peckham, Matt. *NASA-Funded 3D Food Printer: Could It End World Hunger?* 2013. http://newsfeed.time.com/2013/05/24/nasa-funded-3d-food-printer-could-it-end-world-hunger/.

60 Jaybridge. *Jaybridge Robotics Partners with Kinze Manufacturing.* 2011. http://www.jaybridge.com/news/story/?p=116.

61 Oxford University. *Robot Sheepdog Project.* 2001. http://www.cs.ox.ac.uk/stephen.cameron/sheepdog/.

62 Kremer, Ken. *Curiosity Rover Testing in Harsh Mars-like Environment.* 2011. http://www.universetoday.com/84284/curiosity-rover-testing-in-harsh-mars-like-environment/.

63 MacKenzie, Angus. *Ultra-Ever Dry hydrophobic coating repels almost any liquid.* 2013. http://www.gizmag.com/hydrophobic-coating-repels-liquids/26286/.

64 Dwyer, Jim. *One Tunnel, Two Views of the Future.* 2008. http://www.nytimes.com/2008/09/24/nyregion/24about.html.

65 Jester. *Hasler Self Steering.* http://www.jesterinfo.org/haslerselfsteering.html.

66 Handwerk, Brian. *Giant Robotic Cages to Roam Seas as Future Fish Farms?* . 2009.

http://news.nationalgeographic.com/news/2009/08/090818-giant-robotic-fish-farms.html.

67 U.S. Census Bureau. "Current Population Survey." 2011.

68 Iannelli, Vincent. *Child Abuse Statistics.* 2013. http://pediatrics.about.com/od/childabuse/a/05_abuse_stats.htm.

69 Alper, Meryl. *"There's a nap for that!": YouTube videos of young children using Apple devices.* 2011. http://merylalper.com/2011/10/16/theres-a-nap-part-two/.

70 Biémont, Christian, and Cristina Vieira. "Junk DNA as an evolutionary force." *Nature,* 2006.

71 Miller, Ross. *Fujitsu's social robot bear is the supertoy of Kubrick's dreams, almost.* 2010. http://www.engadget.com/2010/10/05/fujitsus-social-robot-bear-is-the-supertoy-of-kubricks-dreams/.

72 The Associated Press. *Some schools grouping students by skill, not grade level.* 2010. http://usatoday30.usatoday.com/news/education/2010-07-05-grade-held-back_N.htm.

73 Bruner, Jon. *Will online learning destroy America's colleges?* 2012. http://radar.oreilly.com/2012/11/online-learning-college-mooc.html.

74 Gabriel, Trip. *More Pupils Are Learning Online, Fueling Debate on Quality.* 2011. http://www.nytimes.com/2011/04/06/education/06online.html?pagewanted=all.

75 Barseghian, Tina. *Three Trends That Define the Future of Teaching and Learning.* 2011. http://blogs.kqed.org/mindshift/2011/02/three-trends-that-define-the-future-of-teaching-and-learning/.

76 Melanson, Donald. *Mr. Asahi robot bartender makes its public debut.* 2008. http://www.engadget.com/2008/07/02/mr-asahi-robot-bartender-makes-its-public-debut/.

77 PRWeb. *Self Serve Table Taps and Beer Walls Create New Ways for People to Drink and Enjoy Draft Beer.* 2012. http://www.prweb.com/releases/Tabletaps/Ellickson/prweb9097495.htm.

78 Stewart, Lorna. *Why do radiologists miss dancing gorillas?* 2013. http://www.bbc.co.uk/news/health-21466529.

79 Booen, B. *The Top 10 Automated Warehouses.* 2011. http://www.supplychaindigital.com/warehousing_storage/top-10-automated-warehouses.

80 Economides, Steve. *America's Cheapest Family Gets You Right on the Money.* Three Rivers Press, 2007.

81 Mlot, Stephanie. *Apple Stores Top Tiffany's in Retail Sales Per Square Foot.* 2012. http://www.pcmag.com/article2/0,2817,2412094,00.asp.

82 *Average Weekly Work Hours.* Bureau of Labor Statistics, 2010.

83 Yee, Lee Chyen, and Clare Jim. *Foxconn to rely more on robots; could use 1 million in 3 years.* 2011. http://www.reuters.com/article/2011/08/01/us-foxconn-robots-

idUSTRE77016B20110801.

84 Diamond, Jared. *What's Your Consumption Factor?* 2008. http://www.nytimes.com/2008/01/02/opinion/02diamond.html?pagewanted=all.

85 Oremus, Will. *North Carolina May Ban Tesla Sales To Prevent "Unfair Competition"*. 2013. http://www.slate.com/blogs/future_tense/2013/05/13/north_carolina_tesla_ban_bill_would_prevent_unfair_competition_with_car.html.

86 Mack, Eric. *iPhone manufacturing costs revealed?* 2012. http://news.cnet.com/8301-17938_105-57382995-1/iphone-manufacturing-costs-revealed/.

87 Kavoussi, Bonnie. *Average Cost Of A Factory Worker In The U.S., China And Germany*. 2012. http://www.huffingtonpost.com/2012/03/08/average-cost-factory-worker_n_1327413.html.

88 Kavoussi, Bonnie. *Average Cost Of A Factory Worker In The U.S., China And Germany*. 2012. http://www.huffingtonpost.com/2012/03/08/average-cost-factory-worker_n_1327413.html.

89 Mcor Technologies. *Staples' First 3D Printing 'Experience Centre' Goes LiveMcor Technologies.* 2013. http://news.thomasnet.com/companystory/Staples-First-3D-Printing-Experience-Centre-Goes-Live-Powered-by-Mcor-Technologies-20007559.

90 Shapeways. *Are You Ready to 3D Print Electronics on to Your 3D Printed Designs?* 2013.

http://www.shapeways.com/blog/archives/1922-are-you-ready-to-3d-print-electronics-on-to-your-3d-printed-designs.html.

91 Brandrick, Chris. *3D Printers Now Print Human Body Parts.* 2012. http://www.techhive.com/article/249359/3d_printer_now_prints_human_body_parts.html.

92 Rubens, Paul. *3D printing: A new dimension to faking it.* 2013. http://www.bbc.com/future/story/20130208-a-new-dimension-to-faking-it/2.

93 Greenberg, Andy. *3D-Printing Firm Makerbot Cracks Down On Printable Gun Designs.* 2012. http://www.forbes.com/sites/andygreenberg/2012/12/19/3d-printing-startup-makerbot-cracks-down-on-printable-gun-designs/.

94 National Academies. *Medication Errors Injure 1.5 Million People and Cost Billions of Dollars Annually.* 2006. http://www8.nationalacademies.org/onpinews/newsitem.aspx?RecordID=11623.

95 Intuitive Surgical. *Regulatory Clearance.* 2011. http://www.intuitivesurgical.com/specialties/regulatory-clearance.html.

96 Singer, Emily. *The Slow Rise of the Robot Surgeon.* 2010. http://www.technologyreview.com/news/418141/the-slow-rise-of-the-robot-surgeon/.

97 Lohr, Steve. *I.B.M.'s Watson Goes to Medical School.* 2012. http://bits.blogs.nytimes.com/2012/10/30/i-b-m-s-watson-goes-to-medical-school/.

98 Freeland, Chrystia. *The Problems of a Graying Population.* 2011. http://www.nytimes.com/2011/07/29/world/americas/29iht-letter29.html.

99 Locker, Melissa. *MIT Researchers Create Star Trek-Style Needleless Injections.* 2012. http://newsfeed.time.com/2012/05/30/mit-invents-star-trek-needleless-injections/.

100 Libin, Alexander V., and Elena V. Liben. "Person–Robot Interactions From the Robopsychologists' Point of View: The Robotic Psychology and Robotherapy Approach." *PROCEEDINGS OF THE IEEE*, 2004.

101 News Medical. *Animal robots help treat dementia.* 2013. http://www.news-medical.net/news/20130308/Animal-robots-help-treat-dementia.aspx.

102 *Frost & Sullivan Recognizes Compliance Meds Technologies' CleverCap.* 2013. http://online.wsj.com/article/PR-CO-20130416-906635.html.

103 Fung, Brian. *The $289 Billion Cost of Medication Noncompliance, and What to Do About It.* 2012. http://www.theatlantic.com/health/archive/2012/09/the-289-billion-cost-of-medication-noncompliance-and-what-to-do-about-it/262222/.

104 —. *RIBA-II healthcare robot now stronger, smarter -- still a bear.* 2011. http://www.engadget.com/2011/08/02/riba-ii-healthcare-robot-now-stronger-smarter-still-a-bear/.

105 Harris, Mark. *Emotion sensing robots can tell how you feel.*

2009. http://www.techradar.com/us/news/world-of-tech/emotion-sensing-robots-can-tell-how-you-feel-532813.

106 Abbott, Alison. *http://www.nature.com/news/brain-simulation-and-graphene-projects-win-billion-euro-competition-1.12291.* 2013. Brain-simulation and graphene projects win billion-euro competition.

107 Blain, Loz. *The serious truth behind the adorable PARO baby seal-bot.* 2010. http://www.gizmag.com/paro-robot-baby-seal-companion/13753/.

108 World Psychiatric Association. *Early Detection and Management of Mental Disorders.* 2004: Wiley, 2004.

109 Fritz, Justin. *Wall St Daily.* 2011. http://www.wallstreetdaily.com/2011/04/12/telemedicine-healthcare/.

110 Brain S. Alper, M.D., M.S.P.H. *Curbside Consultation.* 2006. http://www.aafp.org/afp/2006/0801/p482.html.

111 Dolan, Brian. *Which sensors are coming to your next smartphone?* 2011. http://mobihealthnews.com/11006/which-sensors-are-coming-to-your-next-smartphone/.

112 Szondy, David. *Healthspot replaces doctor's office with a telepresence kiosk.* 2013. http://www.gizmag.com/healthspot/25972/.

113 R&D Mag. *Engineering team improves lab-on-a-chip blood testing technology.* 2012. http://www.rdmag.com/news/2012/09/engineering-team-improves-lab-chip-blood-testing-technology.

114 ABC. *How Uninsured Americans Affect Your Care.* 2012. http://abcnews.go.com/GMA/DrJohnson/story?id=128240&page=1#.Ua-pGvZAT8Y.

115 Paur, Jason. *UAV in a Firefight of a Different Kind.* 2009. http://www.wired.com/autopia/2009/08/firefighting-uav/.

116 Saletan, William. *Chess Bump.* 2007. http://www.slate.com/articles/health_and_science/human_nature/2007/05/chess_bump.html.

117 Lyman, Rick. *Movie Stars Fear Inroads By Upstart Digital Actors.* 2001. http://www.nytimes.com/2001/07/08/us/movie-stars-fear-inroads-by-upstart-digital-actors.html?pagewanted=all&src=pm.

118 Osterhout, Jacob E. *Rapper Tupac Shakur hits stage at Coachella with the help of 3-D technology Read more: http://www.nydailynews.com/entertainment/music-arts/back-dead-rapper-tupac-returns-stage-coachella-3-d-technology-article-1.1062595#ixzz2VNhWXmt7.* 2012. http://www.nydailynews.com/entertainment/music-arts/back-dead-rapper-tupac-returns-stage-coachella-3-d-technology-article-1.1062595.

119 France-Presse, Agence. *Robot artist learns masters' brush strokes.* 2012. http://www.mnn.com/green-tech/gadgets-electronics/stories/robot-artist-learns-masters-brush-strokes.

120 Ortiz, Christina. *Robot Paints Your Sleep Pattern.* 2012. http://news.discovery.com/tech/ibis-robot-paints-dreams-121017.htm.

121 Lee, Jesse. *Behind the Scenes: President Obama and Disney's*

*Hall of Presidents.* 2009.
http://www.whitehouse.gov/blog/2009/07/02/behind-scenes-president-obama-and-disneys-hall-presidents.

122 Quick, Darren. *Disney Research robot can juggle, play catch.* 2012. http://www.gizmag.com/disney-catching-robot/25145/.

123 Saygin, Ayse Pinar, Ilyas Cicelkli, and Varol Akman. *Turing Test: 50 Years Later.* Kluwer, 2001.

124 White, Ronald D. *Bionic eye maker has vision of the future.* 2013. http://articles.latimes.com/2013/apr/27/business/la-fi-made-in-california-eye-20130428.

125 Heaven, Douglas. *First mind-reading implant gives rats telepathic power.* 2013.
http://www.newscientist.com/article/dn23221-first-mindreading-implant-gives-rats-telepathic-power.html.

126 Lupkin, Sydney. *Aimee Copeland Gets Bionic Hands.* 2013. http://abcnews.go.com/blogs/health/2013/05/17/aimee-copeland-gets-bionic-hands/.

127 Daily Mail. *Goodbye wheelchair: Bionic legs allow paralysed man to walk again.* 2010.
http://www.dailymail.co.uk/sciencetech/article-1295024/Bionic-legs-let-paralysed-man-walk-again.html.

128 Caddick, Amy. *The real-life cyborg - getting to know Professor Kevin Warwick.* 2012.
http://www.scienceomega.com/article/454/the-real-life-cyborg-getting-to-know-professor-kevin-warwick.

129 Lin, Judy. *Research shows that Internet is rewiring our brains.* 2008. http://www.today.ucla.edu/portal/ut/081015_gary-small-ibrain.aspx.

130 Bosker, Bianca. *Google Glass Privacy Concerns Spurred Lawmakers To Ask Larry Page These 8 Questions.* 2013. http://www.huffingtonpost.com/2013/05/17/google-glass-privacy-concerns-lawmakers_n_3292301.html.

# INDEX

## A



## B

C

## E



## F

G



H

## I



## J

K



L



M

N



O



P

## S

## T

facebook.com/Jobocalypse

@TheJobocalypse

My biggest secret, encrypted for your enjoyment.

hQIOAyamjyWmVrxREAf+JRwQucKLNoR6+CW/PCZhmbb0LCW2a3wA/frQjyu93dk
M/oAqqJK8+8h1N3md/UW51ugLs5K84yUJ1As4/ey9AJb8dOrsMaYXl9Jb/dg4XvfU
8xxCwOt7vAfQuAdmaAB/ThoX7mBFsTjhpVU6JP10VFv9NC6lfDntQIWMiADy/YJ5
vtxTm4DFD3V4I72fJKxK06e7iynzh07AgT9fDE+79fSI5Y/i/iqjnRePyxFLBYJL
iHN2Mr2jwQSCeI/ij6merrqYHeGpullTtX74IqSlGgZFfl4oC2tCHn14SsjYGHpP
QRH8+/i5lgNrgHuvGlBsSZRz/GhDgGnS4q54oNizFAf+LbCkLrhrLcEGhSuQ+Sj9
c15PgHfxNvyoE4XmTne8coW3dFIOp9m/hF+CNCJHC28a1g2OOHTK5ZncVj4MGo74
75fCaA4DwX1M48Y5HDE53YdL0fdrx/ep/uyIgfgXpKK3UOtrM8dEfm66hmz69PXO
rNuLEivA0nzuy0GBpLdOonOXpIlz4pzY+hvbXkUZ+gg0WBA3mOaTvz04HZKzsdyh
h/YZ63rnLf2dpn6kIluoxmvPm4CjFe9V8iZicr482D/kRWFA/abIlPpXHp3a8/s6
KBomj9YB/AATKvjjPZLsWxkXXMvUQxkRq4zZJk1lBZqNFThgozpPfvzvcjdnLj9I
7NLqAVw4I7/lgnmjGB3J8hQLaTG/z5rzN8QRNO7e7DNfkXsd5ekFGqIeC61tu2eL
0rH/6Y2fkRJhTPsnmaVwko34y2OuCt/CUcHZ156f8mPa5Tu/5ec6TZ/ic9YtahbW
yRch1HsYypuQ2U1oS42fc9wMkxnTkWSMGjMZB23IAYrWFGSZ2KcZl3KPZESuuKCL
NbuaLIRvCSbtJF2gOJvk1DkJebpi3daX663lUkVnihKO4jK/ZBmrCBtiA5BgbHqP
H3RBFXxJophkc1DZRMX/euNeuRP30QRWNV3Hv1r2EAhKZ3o/VKJxUCjtKfTnSZCE
0TB0P3D2x6G0/R+iiYXRYVtKlzVvpACxEux1cCjUsFJrZaqA7hozx4kxDsHH8XBK
aim4fC9ieoGknJTg3AF7egUx/s9dTYDw7mrFybRT35By+gxhIF5jl/nMLM6v6ewv
/8SMBMm49FP5dfLgzwgL2LHEZfTaujJ5jTQOMmaag/KyvL5E4eMiydlj36qJfhRT
ytwklegZ93WziE/0U6c1E6TWG3dpbL1rmJ6bJGQI9IC0f+IyBFy+h13Cew0+kmga
9x9zcJ+t5v9OHDoyQmkQAIrx0JkQ9Y75/6iQgXhP3IB0y+jKIXKj7xFZWcs7RCS5
vAl1zUDmYil/7wHZ2mLi6e5EMDRKhQZG8KLwoerUjGl7Q7UjlldlaQhWi5wg/6lX
addYJ5Er0K1qDZAcPab7DWyEf79lEFMm/epCED3DSrnSY2G+/vjolS+Sw5CuqnwO
qvPXoNmeBOXTgsS6HPwu6OODjeYAGAoMcXHmhdz+ERFAnBTD3yIxo+P5ZWFNi
klUGQ234QDoutwFVrwZMEdf4V1CHtzygKj7mHWhKp5ttBWJLqVko/nnmJX0GYHL
nKHtU3sc9N13e5/hbPkYhDvwNhBIyN1FeRp/SA/uFeYZWsOq7LAXZrs6WHhZDE+4
B0dDZyMAIS6zXqmiNfuw62V1jv2ouC/+xusqIDt/3HlH8bhkXdqwAeCU8qk7BC7D08P
Ch8Jkk52y4l2iaGIRo3bVGOXyL50AW6SKVUPwX6HPSC2XQu9xMEzQKMEvYUxI19
N0b7dqpYCJdcYu1AXiWFlJtXgSb7RvQPSjZXp9zoHaL9n0gP3p2Xj16D76bjOjxTmY
+BcXzM9DT9K63z6cWXPfIyI070PX5iN3Gn3flgf6ijF4DGQo0ldnF7xvxmZHxtXS
k4sHIJLTyzvdVWE6Hs2TgcZloiN7h8TOuf89QVdU2Pe9Q2ea4lTHA1Nidx5pEWNe
wHYeuL7xR5Hk0AevptsI8Q+SoOiRvOaDhpaKUmpZBcVk68NV9e40NUpteifMLI9Y
Uz5orrEuMc37bhlvnL//ZlfaiMDI8uBaiKR+W4GRSgTCILErSoo9JLq564NSXXLP
YKDvkqWpoi9KWqg9L11ZVUbFYDSjQAikdXkktkBbH6hK6GxZjFlMb+5p8Q1uGwBw
Joc0JCOsN+SBMHfJy92BUWOXMpWjSaRtKDy2//xT2nwLvgN8u39FHK+Py8QxeDYq
yHV0uyKj1IHucwfbNBa0y9a2xNFlXqxgSq0F5ZMqoEhqeu/OWEWFGiMd+K/84cuJ
2358ajPtIFaSrDraP9ngDKvXWjiageslrhj+izpM/jw1ulCjrAfy+7xG9Q64Ef3W
8PP9ivLcgTWRdiRx2XCkN+wnNPUlgvILr/1jCm+WOc52QuJjQmi+af12CKg4kMKq
FKyX7wZT5lXf6PWFBhRxc/djS59ZJ0DIUENcmiMEcB4Qtyb+1oIyT+WizFfU4BHR
bIeWddcO2uHWLUVANFUnuCZui2fvQRh0Da3uvdF48VWSwqsgWZ/UFZdSmH+9e
MLD0jqq+vwIAFdgrhoh6z+P+nvAKAA4ILicc+Gr/k8==w/uw

28846081R00103

Made in the USA
Lexington, KY
03 January 2014